D1051043

HOMEBASE

HOMEBASE

A NOVEL

SHAWN WONG

UNIVERSITY OF WASHINGTON PRESS

Seattle & London

The author wishes to thank the Mary Roberts Rinehart Foundation for their support, Him Mark Lai for his translations of Angel Island Poetry, Edmund Ow for his Angel Island research, Lane Publishing Company for permission to quote from the *Sunset Western Garden Book*, and Kay Boyle for permission to quote from her poem "Branded for Slaughter."

Various portions of this novel were first published in *Aiiieeeee! An Anthology of Asian American Writers*, *Counterpoint*, and *Yardbird Reader*, vols. 3 and 5.

UNIVERSITY OF WASHINGTON PRESS

PO Box 50096

Seattle, WA 98145–5096

www.washington.edu/uwpress

LIBRARY OF CONGRESS CATALOGING-IN-PUBLICATION DATA

Wong, Shawn, 1949–

Homebase : a novel / Shawn Wong.

— 1st University of Washington Press ed.

p. cm.

ISBN 978-0-295-98816-0

(pbk. : alk. paper)

1. Chinese Americans—Fiction. I. Title.

PS3573.O583H66 2008

813'.54—dc22   2007050329

The paper used in this publication is acid-free and 90 percent recycled from at least 50 percent post-consumer waste. It meets the minimum requirements of American National Standard for Information Sciences-Permanence of Paper for Printed Library Materials, ANSI Z39.48–1984.

For Frankie and Kay

AILANTHUS altissima (A. *glandulosa*). Tree-of-Heaven.
Deciduous tree. All Zones. Native to China. Planted a
century ago in California's gold country where it now runs
wild. . . . Inconspicuous greenish flowers are usually followed
by handsome clusters of red-brown, winged fruits in late summer and fall. . . . Often condemned as a weed tree because it
suckers profusely, but it must be praised for its ability to create
beauty and shade under adverse conditions—drought, hot
winds, and every type of difficult soil.

—*Sunset Western Garden Book*

He was frozen to death in the snow.
He was going to drown himself in the bay.
After searching for several days they caught the murderer.
Did they find anything in his possession?
They did.
He was killed by an assassin.
He tried to assassinate me.
He tried to kill me by assassination.
He is an assaulter.
He was smothered in his room.
He was suffocated in his room.
He was shot dead by his enemy.
He was poisoned to death by his friend.
He tries to kill him by poisoning.
He tries to inflict death by poison.
Assault with the intention to do bodily injury.
He took the law in his own hand.
He tried to deprive me of my wages.
I go home at night.
I have gone home.
I went home.
I abide at home.
I abode at San Francisco.
I have lived in Oakland.

> —*An English-Chinese Phrase Book*
> Also, A Complete List of Wells Fargo & Co.'s
> Offices in California, Nevada, Etc.,
> Compiled by Wong Sam and Assistants, 1875.

INTRODUCTION
TO THE UNIVERSITY OF
WASHINGTON PRESS EDITION

WRITERS ARE NOT VERY GOOD AT WRITING ABOUT THEIR OWN work. Over the years excerpts of *Homebase* have been reprinted in textbooks and often there is a set of discussion questions about the meaning of the selection. When I read the questions, I pause to think about how to answer them. What usually first comes to mind is what I was doing when I wrote that section of the book rather than any kind of sophisticated literary analysis. If the publisher sends me the teacher's edition, I look up the answers and sometimes say to myself, "Wow, that makes sense. I'll have to remember that the next time I talk about my novel."

A few years ago, *Homebase* was chosen as the freshman book at Whitman College and I was asked to submit a list of discussion questions. I was at such a loss to think of any questions that I sent e-mails to several professors who use *Homebase* as a text and asked them to send me their discussion and exam questions. (Those questions are at the end of the book as there's no teacher's edition).

In this introduction to the new edition of *Homebase*, I'll stick to the how and why of its publication rather than explore, as many introductions do, the scholarly meaning of the work. The literary history of this novel is important because it came out of my knowledge of Asian American literary history as do all my books. Why is this important?

Ten years ago I was approached by a young graduate student who was writing part of her PhD dissertation on *Homebase*. I was, of course, flattered and asked about her theoretical approach to the work. She said that, in her mind, *Homebase* was paternalistic and represented my efforts to legitimize the Asian American masculinist position. I thought for a moment before speaking. Should I simply say thank you for your opinion of my book or should I declaw the literary jargon on the spot? I'm a professor so I took the educational position.

"That's interesting. How many Asian American novels have you read?"

"Five."

"Why would you say my work is paternalistic?"

"Your novel only has male characters and deals mainly with issues of Chinese American male identity."

I decided to work with that number. "You've read five novels. Do you realize that when *Homebase* was first published in 1979, it was the only Chinese American work of literary fiction in print in America?"

She shrugged. The 1970s were probably closer to the ice age than her world.

I began again. "If you were a Chinese American novelist and you knew when you were writing your novel that there were no novels by a Chinese American in print in America, what do you think you would write or what do you think your job would be?"

My voice had changed from writer meeting fan to professor giving lecture. "In fact, when I started writing *Homebase* in the late '60s, there were one or two obscure books about Chinese in America in print. And, the only two works of literary fiction were Diana Chang's *The Frontiers of Love*, originally published in 1956, and Louis Chu's *Eat a Bowl of Tea*, originally published in 1961, and both were currently out of print."

I was on a roll now. "Well, maybe your job would be to educate an audience about something called Chinese American literature and Chinese American history. *Homebase* is, in part, a work of historical fiction. Why are most of the characters male in the book?" I didn't wait for an answer. "The early Chinese immigrants to America were mostly male and racist immigration laws later created a bachelor society in America. Therefore, it is wrong to dismiss *Homebase* as being masculinist and paternalistic without first knowing the historical context—both the literary history of Asian America and the history in the story. In addition, by focusing only on your point of view of the book as paternalistic, you're completely ignoring one of the major characters in the novel—the mother."

I stopped my impromptu "lecture." At public readings, I am most often asked whether my work is autobiographical. I usually say it is a work of fiction with autobiographical elements so that I don't have to get into facts about my life. But, the reality is *Homebase* is a story about my mother and father and it hurt me to hear that the student hadn't considered the role of the mother in my novel or worse, ignored her for the sake of cramming my novel into her literary theory. I wrote the book for my mother and father, to honor their lives. My father died when I was seven and my mother died when I was fifteen. Neither one lived passed their fortieth birthday. I wanted to tell the graduate student that by ignoring the character of the mother in *Home-base* she was using a pair of scissors and cutting her out of my family portrait.

At the other end of the spectrum of reader responses, I once received a letter from a reader who didn't mention any aspect of the historical parts of the novel dealing with Chinese American immigration and the building of the Central Pacific railroad over the Sierra Nevada mountains. Instead, she simply wrote that reading my novel helped her understand how to handle grief. That kind of intimate and personal response and the fact that the novel is still being read thirty years after its publication is very gratifying.

When I was an eighteen-year-old freshman at San Francisco State College (now San Francisco State University) in 1967, I took a beginning poetry writing class from James Liddy, an Irish poet (now at the University of Wisconsin-Milwaukee). I had been writing poetry for several months and I thought I was already a poet and taking the class would only confirm the fact. Once I was enrolled in the class I realized very quickly that I was a terrible poet. Professor Liddy never told me I was a terrible poet—he didn't have to—but he did encourage me. By the time the semester ended, I was a better poet and I wanted to *be* a poet. The following year I worked on my writing one-on-one with Kay Boyle and that was the beginning of a twenty-four-year relationship between us until her death in 1992. At various times she was my teacher, mentor, friend, and for a period in the early '70s while in graduate school, I rented a room from her in her four-story Victorian house in San Francisco's Haight-Ashbury district (rent was $70 a month). She taught me not only how to be a writer, but also how to live one's life as a writer. The house was filled with artifacts and memorabilia from her days living in Paris and elsewhere in Europe in the 1920s. One day I came home with a copy of the *Dubliners* tucked under my arm and she said to me, while we were both checking the mail, "I see you're reading Jim's book." A constant stream of writers, singers, artists, journalists, teachers, community activists, and even letters from Samuel Beckett entered through the front door of her house at 419 Frederick Street. Kay taught me that writing "was about belief" and that everything I write needed to be relevant to our lives. In graduate school, she converted me from a somewhat abstract language poet to a novelist and, in the process, I discovered my narrative voice. The first version of this work began as a twenty-page poem.

Homebase is dedicated, in part, to Kay and her last published book, *The Collected Poems of Kay Boyle* (1991), is dedicated to me with the following inscription:

> This book, both in spirit and substance, is for you, Shawn; for you are my second son, as I cherish and respect you, and rejoice in our friendship. It is you who wrote of your mother's death: "I did not want everyone's pity for an orphaned fifteen-year-old boy . . . after she died I was no longer anyone's son. . . ." This is not quite true (although a little late) to call you mine."

It was true that Kay's writing and my writing during the two and half decades I knew her were linked as she described in "spirit and substance." Several passages from *Homebase*, prior to its publication appeared in several of her poems, non-fiction essays, and even in a novel, *The Underground Woman* (1975). *Homebase*, of course, has Kay's influence and mentorship on every page. An earlier version of *Homebase* was my creative writing Master's thesis and I treasure the pages and pages of handwritten notes she provided on this novel and other writings throughout our friendship.

If you went to college in the late 1960s as I did, campuses were in turmoil over the Vietnam war, civil rights, and establishment of ethnic studies on college campuses. In my second year, San Francisco State exploded into daily demonstrations and when various college presidents refused to bring police on campus, they were all fired or resigned until S. I. Hayakawa was installed as president of the college and he brought police on campus. Riots broke out and students were arrested and beaten. Students went on strike. The campus closed down. One day, Kay stood defiantly between protesting students and police. She was not only a mentor to students, but also our protector. Disgusted with S. I. Hayakawa, I transferred to UC Berkeley in 1969, which was, of course, like jumping from the frying pan directly into the fire. Even though I left San Francisco State, I continued to work with Kay and stayed enrolled as a part-time student there while going to school as a full-time student at Berkeley. After I graduated in 1971, I went back to SF State, entered graduate school in creative writing, and moved in with Kay. I did work with other writers while in school—Herb Wilner, Leo Litwak, Stan Rice, and Jackson Burgess (at Berkeley), and even took a class from saxophonist John Handy—but none were as influential as Kay as teacher and editor.

When I started writing in college, I realized one day that I was the *only* Asian American writer I knew in the world and that no teacher in high school or college had ever assigned or even mentioned a book written by an Asian American writer.

The whole field of study called Asian American studies was just being formed at San Francisco State and UC Berkeley. It was Kay Boyle who introduced me to the first Asian American writer I ever met. Jeffery Chan was one of her graduate students and teaching in the newly formed Asian American Studies Department at SF State. When I met Jeff, he gave me the phone number of Frank Chin who lived just a few blocks from me in Berkeley. The three of us found poet Lawson Inada and eventually the four of us co-edited *Aiiieeeee! An Anthology of Asian American Writers* (1974). The publication of *Aiiieeeee!* marked the beginning of the rediscovery of Asian American literature. Franklin Odo, editor of *The Columbia Documentary History of the Asian American Experience* (2002) called the anthology "a pathbreaking work of Asian American literature" and listed the preface to the anthology as one of 155 key historical documents of Asian American history from 1790 to 2001.

Also in 1969, Frank Chin introduced me to writer Ishmael Reed and Ishmael introduced me to a whole range of writers such as Victor Hernandez Cruz, Alex Haley, Al Young, Jessica Hagedorn, Leslie Silko, Ntosake Shange, and even musicians like David "Fat Head" Newman and George Clinton and Funkadelic. Ishmael later founded the Before Columbus Foundation, a literary organization dedicated to the promotion of American multicultural literature, where I served as one of the founding board members in the mid-70s and continue to serve on the board of directors today. Most of this activity happened when I was still in school. Imagine, as an undergraduate student at Berkeley: I was studying the dead white British authors—sitting in Spenser class, writing papers about Chaucer—and outside of class, I was encountering all of the exciting literary life going on in and around the San Francisco Bay Area. In fact, I think my real education was out in the arts and literary communities of the Bay Area where there were no grades, no credit, and no classes.

During my senior year at Berkeley, I took a job as editor of the Glide Urban Center newsletter, which was part of Glide Memorial Methodist Church. I doubt if there was any place in the Bay Area more exciting than Glide in 1971—it was the hub of community activism lead by the dynamic and charismatic Rev. Cecil Williams with Janice Mirikitani as the executive director of Glide Urban Center. It was Mirikitani who first invited me to read my poetry to an audience.

While still in graduate school in 1972, I was offered my first teaching job in the newly formed Ethnic Studies Department at Mills College in Oakland. The dean of the faculty at the time asked me what I could teach and I answered that I could teach a class in Asian American literature. I was offered the job even though I did not have any teaching experience, a graduate degree or any publications, and I was about to teach a subject that I did not learn in college, rather had taught myself. At the time, I was working as a part-time gardener to support myself, so I had a decision to make. I could continue working as a gardener or teach at a private women's college. I was twenty-two and single; I took the job. Jeff, Frank, Lawson, and I had completed the manuscript of *Aiiieeeee!* and I used that as the foundation for the course.

After several trade publishers turned down *Aiiieeeee!*, Howard University Press decided to publish the anthology as part of their inaugural list of ten books in 1974. It instantly became the most reviewed book on their list with reviews in every newspaper and periodical from *The New York Times* to *Rolling Stone* to *The New Yorker. Aiiieeeee!* was later published in paperback by Doubleday.

I graduated from San Francisco State in the same year and started circulating *Homebase* around to publishers with no success. Ishmael Reed and Kay Boyle both introduced my book to various editors at large publishing houses, but all turned it down. While waiting to publish the novel, I rewrote it eight times, each time making the language in the novel work harder and using my training in poetry to get the most out the narrative. Finally, in 1979, Ishmael decided to publish the book himself with his own small press, I. Reed Books. The novel won two literary awards and was later published by Plume, a division of Penguin Books. In 1975, Frank Chin and I co-edited an edition of *The Yardbird Reader*, a literary journal started by Ishmael Reed, Al Young, and other African American writers and artists. It was no accident that my first three books were published by African American publishers. They were the first to recognize the legitimacy of Asian American literature.

In the early '70s Frank, Jeff, Lawson, and I formed the Combined Asian-American Resources Project, Inc. (CARP) dedicated to the rediscovery of Asian American literature and preserving oral history interviews with writers and artists. Our CARP oral history interviews are collected at UC Berkeley's Bancroft Library. When we couldn't find a publisher to reprint John Okada's landmark 1957 novel, *No-No Boy*, we used our own money, borrowed money from several sources, and published a new edition in 1976. *No-No Boy* was published by the University of Washington Press in 1979 and recently sold its 100,000th copy.

The literary history cited here is, of course, not just about one novel, but rather about the dissemination, preservation, and promotion of a whole field of literature. As a young writer, who started writing *Homebase* almost forty years ago, I realized very early on that I was responsible for educating an audience to Asian American writing as well as for writing it.

SHAWN WONG
Seattle, Washington
November 2007

HOMEBASE

CHAPTER ONE

I

BACK IN THE EARLY FIFTIES, WHEN I WAS FOUR, MY FATHER AND
mother drove from Berkeley to New York and back. The sound
of the car's little engine is still buzzing and working away in my
head. My sense of balance comes from lying asleep in the back
seat of that car, my unsteady heartbeat comes from my father's
night driving and my watching the chaos of passing headlights
floating by on our car's ceiling and gleaming tail-lights reflected
and distorted in the windows. In those nights, sleeping in the back
seat of my father's car, I heard conversations my mother and father
had, saw places I visited later, and remembered it all when I started
driving. And the places I've never been to before were dreams,
were whole conversations my father and mother had.

I will eventually travel to all the places I've dreamed about.
I will meet my friends and know them as if I'd known them all
my life.

I was named after my great-grandfather's town, the town he
first settled in when he came to California from China: Rains-

SHAWN WONG

ford, California. Rainsford Chan (Chan is short for California). Rainsford doesn't exist anymore. There's no record of it ever having existed, but I've heard stories about it. I've spent many days hiking and skiing through the Sierra Nevada looking for it. I've never found exactly where it was, but I'm almost sure I've seen it or passed by it on one of those days. I recognized it from a hill. It was one of those long, wide Sierra meadows. A place of shade. The sound of a stream reaches my ears. Dogwood trees make the place sound like a river when the breeze moves through the leaves.

My father knew all his grandfather's stories about the town or towns like it. Stories of how they survived there, of how they were driven out of the west and chased back to San Francisco. As they rushed back across the land they worked on, they burned their letters, their diaries, poems, anything with names. My father never told me these stories. He died too soon. He only taught me to sing "Home on the Range" and I'd teach him the songs I learned in school. But I knew all his stories because my mother told me all his stories and later I found stories he had written down and put away in an old shoe box.

The year before his death we moved from Berkeley to Guam. In 1956 my mother called the dirt road in front of our house on Guam "Ocean Street," and gave the only house on that street the number "25." We began to receive mail there from home. I was six and until we had moved to Guam I remembered only a few isolated events out of my childhood in Berkeley, where my parents were students. When we returned to Berkeley in 1957, Father was dead. And I remembered everything.

In 1956 my father taught me to sing "Home on the Range" on that island in the Pacific Ocean. Standing there in the heat of an ocean lagoon, I sang out for my father about our home on

4

the range and my friends the buffalo and antelope. The sun was shining, it was raining, and the steam of the humid day filled my lungs. The waves washing up on the edges of the lagoon made the green grass seaweed between my toes.

I must have been calling my father "Bobby" for a few years before we arrived in Guam, but it was there that I actually remember for the first time calling him by that name. I had given him that name when, as a baby, I mispronounced "Daddy." That wasn't his real name, just my name for him, it made him the object of my play, a friend I learned my imagination from. When we lived on Guam, I got the last good look, the last clear view of my family at the age of six. On Guam, my world was a boy's paradise and I remember all of it and its memory is constant. In 1956, World War II was still on for me. If I dug beneath the fallen leaves and loose earth near the base of the tree, I always found gleaming brass bullet casings. And there was a fighter jet in the woods behind our house. It was a world of real aircraft carriers, destroyers, submarines, bombers, sunken ships, and palm-lined white sandy beaches. At night the humid animals of the day, the lizards, insects, and rodents, made a zoo of noises in my sleep.

On this island, the tropical night still hisses its hot breath against my ears. The day must cool into evening, Father. When you and I sat on the front porch, there was no movement to cool the day. I followed my father into the jungle behind our house, the boondocks, the name itself was myth and legend. The enemies of all our life were hiding in the grasses, behind the rubble, a jungle of blood. I knew Jap soldiers were hidden away in the tunnels against the hill, still fighting the war. The terror of my childhood was a crashed and charred fighter-jet lying mangled amid the roots of the trees. Some nights I woke thinking I heard that jet crash into the trees with a noise so great that I knew it was a dream noise—it makes me deaf, but the dream still goes on. In the faint light of that humid night the fighter glowed, lifted itself in my eyes like silver smoke, and brought the taste of metal to my tongue. And I could not stop myself from peering down inside the cockpit, feeling the metal still warm from the burn, reaching down through the broken glass into that old air to brush away the smoke, and finding the broken body of a ghost.

When my father was a young man he tried to climb Mount Shasta in California's north gold country, but was defeated by the wind rushing down the mountain face. My father said the wind was always the conqueror, not the cold, or the snow, or the heat, but the wind that makes you deaf, numbs your touch, and pushes blood into your eyes.

My father was sleeping in a stone cabin at the foot of Mount Shasta and was awakened by the sickening smell of rotting wood and the muted voices of Chinamen. His bed became soiled with the breath of poor men. He was getting sick in the pre-dawn night when a voice spoke to him, "Do you know me?" a woman asked, touching his ears with her hands.

"Yes," he lied, seeing the dim outline of her naked body. His eyes filled with smoke. He tried to breathe. The wood of the room smelled like burning dust as he reached for her.

"Are you afraid of dying with me?" she asked, drawing his hand to her stomach, putting her moist mouth in his ear, making him deaf, his throat ached for the moist moss of trees.

"Yes," he answered, knowing she was the nightmare that made China the bitterness of his grandfather's and father's life. He heard her heart beating in his stomach. He left tears on her breast.

In all the days I visited my father in the hospital when he

was dying, I don't remember a single day in detail. I do not remember what I was doing when he died. I do not remember what day he went into the hospital, how many days he stayed there. What time he died. I never asked. I just knew one day in spring, 1957, it was all over. All I had left was a pile of pictures and some clothes my mother put away for me to wear when I got big enough.

My father is twenty-eight years old in the photo I carry of him. I remember him like that. He is seated in a wooden chair on a lawn somewhere, his legs are crossed, he is looking to his right. It is a settled look and if I try there's an ambitious feeling to the photograph. Perhaps that's because I'm his son. He is wearing a white shirt, dark V-neck sweater, heavy wool pants, checkered socks, and black shoes. The table at his right is also made of wood. It looks like a wooden box standing on one of its sides. There are heart-shaped holes cut in the two ends of the box table. A folded newspaper separates two empty coffee cups on the tabletop. A stone wall behind him divides the photo in half. Longleaf bushes spill over the top of the stone wall behind him. He is not yet a father. He will not be a father for four more years.

My father will always stay the same in that picture. April, 1945. And when I am twenty-eight we will be the same age. It is dangerous to honor your father. It is hard to really love your father. It is easy to respect him. When you are the same age, or even when you grow older than your father, like growing taller than him, your love changes to honor because you yourself would like to be honored. I must simply love him. When a son takes a risk of love, he naturally loves his father. He commits himself to his father. It is a dangerous risk.

In three more years we will be the same age and I will have been to all the places my father had been.

I remember you, Father, now with urgency. It is night and I am more like you than I have ever been. I hear the same sounds of a tropical night, the clicking of insects, the scrape of a lizard's claws on the screen door. Tonight I remember a humid night on Guam when I held your forehead in my small hands as I rode on your shoulders. My hands felt your ears, the shape of your chin, and the shape of your nose until you became annoyed and placed my hands back on your forehead and shifted my weight on your shoulders. It is April.

When I was a boy, my father whispered to me from his hospital bed, "Rainsford, I love you more and more." He cried and I thought he was singing. He was a father to me even when he was dying. He said, "Fathers should confess their youth to their sons. Confess the lovers of their youth."

My mother kept my father's love letters to her. I found the letters in an old box. I saw my mother and father in their youth. I see them as I see myself now. They are the celebration of strength for me.

I was left a father to myself after my father's death. When a son or daughter dies, the parents have another or adopt another child to raise and love. When a family loses a beloved dog, they go out and buy another quickly before the self-pity replaces that life. When a father dies, there is only violence. I am violent. I commit myself to love, saying it is there, but never going further to grasp loving. My real life eludes action. It leaves me a father to myself.

My mother died eight years after my father and it was then that I realized I was my great-grandfather's son and I knew why the label of orphan meant nothing to me. My great-grandfather had begun a tradition of orphaned men in this country and now I realized I was the direct descendant of that original fatherless and motherless immigrant. Now there was a direct line from the first generation to the fourth generation. I was not hampered by the knowledge of China as home. The closest I had come to China was my own mother, who was the daughter of a Chinese dentist, schooled by private tutors in Tientsin in English and Chinese literature, French, piano, ballet, and painting. She married my father in 1947 when she was a student in painting and he was a graduate student in engineering in Berkeley. His life had been the opposite of hers, and the realm of his history and tradition did not resemble hers in any way. But in America they were expected to notice each other and, in fact, to know each other. He was working as a dishwasher at the Blue and Gold Cafeteria when he did notice her, and he dismissed her with his own form of racial arrogance. His traditions and history were deeply rooted like scars, and he remembered only the bitterness of his father and grandfather, and he cultivated his sensibility from the lives of those lonely men. And he noticed her that day simply because she was the same color as he and she was good-looking. They did not meet again until she took a course in drafting, and he was the teaching assistant in the class. When they first met, she spoke to him in Chinese and he told her he didn't understand Chinese.

"You do not understand Chinese?"

"Nope."

The way he said "nope" was all she needed to prod him. She seemed to know what annoyed him. Young Chinese girls from China annoyed him. She was talking to the side of his face. When a man says "nope" it was time to move on, and my father was looking off into the distance, ready to move. She was slowly moving her head, then her shoulders, trying to make him look at her when she spoke.

"You were born here?"

"Yes," he said, looking at her, then looking away at a point in the distance.

"What generation are you?" she asked. Then she added, looking away from him at the same point in the distance, "I have an uncle who came from China to go to school in Pennsylvania and became a dentist in 1917." She paused, feeling him looking at her. "And another uncle who was a Methodist minister in California in 1850." It was a look of impatience.

"I'm third-generation Chinese," he said quickly.

"You are not Chinese." She caught him saying the word "Chinese" a little too forced, like a lie, just to dismiss her questions. And when they looked at each other finally he was half smiling and she was dead serious. She tested his patience.

A few months after they were married, my mother received a letter from her father telling her that China was closed to her, that it was no longer her home. She was now orphaned to this country and to my father. It would still be a few months before he told her about his history and the lives of his grandfathers because, among other things, he had to teach her how to cook.

When I started driving, I used to drive around at night through the hills, through empty streets, just drive around at night to keep from thinking about the pursuit of my own life. To keep from settling down into the dreams of Father and Mother. But in the end my life was nothing unless I pursued their lives, pursued the life of my grandfather, my great-grandfather. I mirrored them at the beginning, shaped everything behind them, told stories about them to myself, read yellowed letters from one to another. I knew more about them than they would have revealed to me if they were alive. I knew more about the love of my father for my mother than most sons know.

II

I AM THE SON OF MY FATHER, MY GRANDFATHERS, AND I HAVE a story to tell about my history, about a moment in the Pacific when I heard myself saying "ever yours." "Ever" is a word that moves like a song, exposing the heart in its tone, never hiding, never patronizing. The word speaks directly, creates form, and has its own voice.

Great-Grandfather built the railroad through the Sierra Nevada in difficult seasons. Night was a time of peace. On warm nights Great-Grandfather would move away from camp to sleep, away from the night workers. There was a river nearby the camp, and farther upstream, the falls. He always walked beside the moonlit river at night, the cascading water glowing white with the reflection made his footsteps visible. And in the windless night he crossed warm pockets of night air, then cool dark spots, but as he moved closer to the sound of the falls, the night air became moist and only cool. His skin tasted the air. It was an uphill hike to the base of the falls and a steeper climb to the top, where he rested, looking down on the fires of camp. He climbed on large granite stones to reach the top of the falls. He began to sweat. The mist from the crashing falls soaked him and mixed with his sweat. The noise was relief from the railroad iron noise of the day. He rested for a moment, looking down into the river's valley. The water appeared vague, uncertain, it became the sound of moonlight, rather than the sound of water rushing through the valley. The moonlit mist carved valleys out of the granite, not the river. The moon made sounds in Great-Grandfather's eyes, made the mist from the falls look like gray smoke floating down the valley, washing out all the details of the canyon walls, losing its night walker in its movement, cooling his exhaustion,

11

and leaving him dreaming a moan out of all his years of living. But he always woke from that easy rest, and demanded that the tradition he passed on be more than a dream and moan of breath. It was his own voice.

Great-Grandfather heard the last anger of his body in late summer, he craved for the violence of bare lighted rooms, that yellow glow to calm himself, that congestion of men without lovers, without families. He knew he was stuck here. In Wyoming, the thunderstorms moved in every day to bring afternoon showers. The raindrops made the dust rise from the ground, filled his nostrils with the smell of moist earth, he felt the ache in his body rise as the dust rises in the wide meadows. His giving in to America, here, was the violence of his soul and he felt it, chased it, and let it overcome him. After the rains, the humidity rose and moist air mixed with the dust the rain had raised. It was a good smell and he bared his chest to that air.

We do not have our women here. My wife is coming to live here. We are staying. Nothing was sweet about those days I lived alone in the city, unless you can find sweetness in that kind of loneliness. I slept in the back of a kitchen by a grimy window where the light and noises of the wet city streets were ground in and out of me like the cold. The bed was so small I could hardly move away from my dreams. And when I awakened with the blue light of the moon shining in, there would be no dreams. That one moment when I wake, losing my dreams, my arms and heart imagining that she was near me moving closer and I float in her movements and light touch. But the blue light and the noise were always there and I would have nothing in my hands.

"I left for San Francisco one month before my brother. In those days, ships were bringing us in illegally. They usually dropped a lifeboat outside the Golden Gate with the Chinese in it. Then the ship steamed in and at night the lifeboat came in quietly to unload. If they were about to be caught, my people were thrown overboard. But, you see, they couldn't swim because they were chained together. My brother died on that night and now his bones are chained to the bottom of the ocean. Now I am fighting to find a place in this country."

My father and I used to drive down a dusty road on that tropical island singing "Home on the Range," the dust pouring through the windows, collecting on the big furry seats of our Buick Super Eight. I followed him on his rounds, checking building sites, riding shotgun, wearing my Superman shirt and a white starched sailor's hat, and carrying a replica of a long-barreled Colt that made my arm ache whenever I lifted it to take aim. And when my father got sick and we had to fly home, I thought of all those jeep rides we went on, running down a dusty road, holding yourself on with both hands, and when we stopped, the dust would catch us and get in my hair and the corners of my mouth. And instead of making you feel dirty, it dried your back. Before we left, mother pulled the Buick into the garage, scraping the side, pinning us in. I crawled out of the window and went for help.

Great-Grandfather's wife was a delicate, yet a strong and energetic lady, insisting in her letters to Great-Grandfather to let her come and join him. The loneliness was overpowering him, yet he resisted her pleas, telling her that life was too dangerous for a woman. "The people and the work move like hawks around me, I feel chained to the ground, unable even to cry for help. The sun blisters my skin, the winters leave me sick, the cold drains us. I look into the eyes of my friends and there is nothing, not even fear."

Upon receiving his letter, Great-Grandmother told her friends that she was leaving to join her husband, saying that his fight to survive was too much for a single man to bear. And so she came and was happy and the hawks had retreated.

She lived in the city and gave birth to a son while Great-Grandfather was still working in the Sierras building the railroad. He wrote to her, saying that the railroad would be finished in six months and he would return to the city and they would live together again as a family.

During the six months, the hawks came back into his vision. "The hawks had people faces laughing as they pulled me apart with their sharp talons, they had no voices, just their mouths flapping open in a yellow hysteria of teeth." He knew that this was the beginning of sickness for his lover, he sensed her trouble and moments of pain, no word from her was necessary. "Your wounds are my wounds," he said in the night. "The hawks that tear our flesh are disturbed by the perfect day, the pure sun that warms the wounds, I am singing and they cannot tear us apart."

She saw the sun as she woke that morning, after waking all night long in moments of pain. The sun was so pure. She thought that this could not be the city, its stench, its noise replaced by this sweet air. She knew that this air, this breath, was her husband's voice. The ground was steaming dry, the humus became her soul, alive and vital with the moving and pushing of growth. She breathed deeply, the air was like sleep uninterrupted by pain, there was no more home to travel to, this moment was everything that loving could give and that was enough. She was complete and whole with that one breath, like the security of her childhood nights, sleeping with mother, wrapping her arms around her, each giving the other the peace of touch. There was a rush of every happiness in her life that she could feel and touch and as she let go, she thought of their son, and the joy of his birth jarred her and she tried desperately to reach out to wake, to hold on to that final fear, to grasp his childhood trust, but the smell of the humus, the moist decaying leaves struck by sunlight and steaming in her dreams was too much, and she was moving too fast into sleep.

Great-Grandfather had dreams and made vows to his son. "I shall take my son away from these hawks who cause me to mourn. My tears leave scars on my face. There is no strength in self-pity. I will take my son away and move deeper into this country."

For Great-Grandfather it was not enough anymore to say he was *longtime Californ'*. He had lost his faith in the land. He fell into deeper depressions, not from mourning his wife's death, but from his loss of faith in the country. He had been defeated when he vowed not to lose ground to the harsh land and cruel people.

The country that accepted Great-Grandfather and his son now rejected them. He sent his son, my grandfather, back to China. The railroad was finished and the Chinese were chased out of the mines. They were allowed to live, but not to marry. The law was designed so that the Chinese would gradually die out, leaving no sons or daughters.

Great-Grandfather stayed in Wyoming. After the transcontinental railroad was finished, the men in the work teams were cut loose to wander through the West. Thousands of Chinese men had no jobs. Some moved to other parts of the country to build the railroad networks, others became migrant farm workers until the unemployed white laborers forced the passage of laws prohibiting the Chinese from working at certain jobs, in certain areas, and finally with the Exclusion Acts, restricting them from entering the country. The Chinese laborers were rounded up and taken back to Chinatown, San Francisco. And if they couldn't be taken back to Chinatown to stay, they were buried where they stood their ground. Great-Grandfather was standing at the eastern edge of the mountains he had worked in, in every season and temperature, and he left a trail of friends lying in the mountains. Wyoming land was different from the Sierra, where he had started.

For Great-Grandfather and the other Chinese who worked through the Sierra seasons on the Central Pacific Railroad, the one conqueror, the one element they feared the most was the wind. The wind did not bring death, but the dread of it in any season was even more powerful than the freezing nights of winter that stiffened the limbs of the sleeping workers, or the summer heat that caused men to pass out, or the fury of the lightning and thunderstorms. After a few hours, the wind makes them deaf, and after a few days of the strong wind, they begin to lose their senses. Hearing goes first, so they talk to themselves while they work, listening to their own voices, just to listen to something that is not the wind, they wrap cloth around their ears. But the wind never lets up. And at night the men can't talk to themselves all night long, can't sing in their sleep. So the wind interrupts their only peace with the loud noise of trees. Their eyes are swollen from the blood pushed into the aching veins of their sight.

Spring 1866

Spring begins in the Sierras with the first thaw in late February, early March. These are months of apprehension for us. Those who are not laying track forward through the mountain passes move back along the track we laid in the hard winter, going from camp to camp, finding the frozen bodies of our lost friends, lost to the winter nights. Men who couldn't keep warm, or were caught in their sleep by the softly falling snow; thick snow that left us invisible by morning.

So we moved back along the tracks, picking up lost tools, lost friends. Spring was a time of mourning. We'd look for spots on the ground where the sun had melted the snow away and begun to thaw the earth. The ground was softer there, soft enough for a shallow grave. When we had walked back a winter season's worth of track, we would remove fallen trees, straighten the track, clear avalanches. The mountains were in a great stage of flux in spring. There were mud slides and avalanches, snow losing its grip in the warming sun. The sound of the earth was a constant dripping, the huge boulders were stained with melting snow, and each day the warm seepage soaked into the frozen earth, and each day our footfalls sank into mud.

The creeks of ice water began flowing now. The land in flux brought back its sounds of birds, leaves, waters, the land began to breathe and melt. Hairy beasts began to stir, awaken. Life was wet, cool. The train began to rust. When the railroad is finished, I will ride back home on a flat car during spring, pay homage to graves, camps, the whole rising of the earth.

My father wrote to my mother, his lover, said, "Dearest darling," like an old movie, an old radio show, out of the melodrama of their love before marriage. He sang it out in his mind as he wrote it down on the brittle onion-skin paper, "Dearest darling," each letter, each word drawn down from a fine point of ink, drawn out to her so that the heart speaks, not the voice. He whispers as in a dream.

Dearest darling,

Having read your letter of Jan. 8, my mind is rather mixed. My thought always follows your words which you told me in your last letter. I don't know how to handle this if you really feel that way. I don't know even how the world seems to me if I lost you. Darling, don't think that way. It is no good for the both of us.

After I read your letter I went out to take a walk. I thought the cold air would do a little good for me. I staggered along the stone paved road. I did not know which direction I should go. I just followed a man whose name I did not know. I walked through the crowded streets. The darkness. I went into a restaurant finally. I drank a bottle of wine. I am not a good drinker. A bottle of wine is too much for me. All I wanted was to forget the present moment. Yes, it really did it. The earth went around before my eyes. I could feel it. I saw the jupiter.

I shall sail homeward at the end of the month.

I saw him out there in the street. The jupiter was a vision of the heart, it was one man's love.

Summer 1866

Summer was the violent season. Everything was routine, every day was routine. And this dullness was what I reacted against, felt it overcoming my spirit, I let the days ride me. The heat made me sweat, and the sweat mixed with the dust we raised. I cannot tell you what we did each day, except to tell you what we did during the season. We laid more track than in other seasons, we cut more trees, we cleared more ground, built tunnels faster, while we grew weaker and weaker.

In 1866 I discovered the sound of granite rock breaking away. We had reached a solid granite buttress and we chipped, blasted, and drilled at the rock day after day. I lost sight of the color of the day in the sun's heat reflecting off the gray granite mountain. We drilled at the rock until we heard a first warning, a low crack, almost a moan, short, quick, that could be heard even in a wind. If you were beneath that sound, that was your signal to move out of the way. The next sound was the shifting scrape of the granite block. The sun saps your energy, tires your muscles faster, facing the sun's glare in the granite rock, the sun's heat weakens your eyesight, but your hearing is centered on that dull sound of a shift, a scrape, just before the granite boulder breaks away from the cliff. It shatters the air with its bulk, hitting the slope a few times in an unobstructed fall toward the river, sometimes snapping off the tops of trees that stand in the way of its fall. There is so much force, weight, and destruction in its movement, yet that whole process occurs without any sound until it hits the river, and even when we see the splash, the sound doesn't reach us for several seconds. Then the sound is disconnected from the whole event. The granite laid bare by the part that broke away reveals its coolness. The air of its cavity smells old, still cold from its glacial years.

When they died, I needed more than my fifteen years to carry me through. There is more violence in forgetting at fifteen. I wanted to go out into the street, walk, drive, run, do anything to forget my love, not their memory. My father's love for my mother grew the longer they were separated by his job and her schooling. In a dark room at night I discovered the letters, blew dust from the envelopes, inspected the stamps, the date, the handwriting. My father spoke to a page, said what he wanted to say to his lover without embarrassment, without hesitation. Again he called her "Dearest darling" in his next letter, when I never heard him call her that in person. He spoke bravely to her heart, as he spoke bravely to their son twenty-five years later in a room alone.

Dearest darling,

This is the fourth letter I sent you from the beginning of the year. I have not heard from you for a long long time. How are you getting along? I hope you had a fine new year's celebration. Remember when we danced all night long at one party a few years ago? I was not a good dancer but you taught me how. I don't think I am a good dancer now. I don't know what I would do if we were invited to a party now. I lost a chance to learn dancing in my school days, because I was always playing ball. If I am not too old now, I hope I can learn to dance from you.

Enclosed is a snapshot which was taken a few days ago. It was in the evening of a winter day. It was unusually cold, you could feel it in the wind. You could see it in the trees and the natural colors of Wisconsin. Behind me is an old style 5–span bridge. It reminds me of a spot back home where we swam and dived into the cool lake. Those happy hours and laughter are still vivid in my mind. I shall leave here soon.

I feel lonely, darling. I keep myself busy, and try to forget my home and you and all the things of the past which make me lonely.

Sometimes I can't help thinking about those happy times and I feel so lonesome.

I will be home soon.

My letters will start somewhere in the Mariposa Grove of redwood trees, Big Trees, Yosemite National Park, where my father brought me and my mother and aunt and uncle. We camped there in the giant shade of those tall trees, counted steps around the base of those trees, drove through the tunnel redwood tree. My father took pictures of me in the driver's seat of that old black Ford. The car was parked in the giant opening of the tree tunnel, and I was standing on the seat with my two hands up high on the steering wheel, my mother was waving from the opposite window at the camera. And in the letter I will write I return there now, renew an acquaintance with cool earth, the smell of brown redwood leaves scattered on the forest floor. I will remember how my father showed me the stump of a once giant redwood tree, showed me its rings of growth. Like a blind man, he made me run my fingers over each year grain to feel the year of my great-grandfather's birth, my grandfather's birth, his own birth, and my birth. Out of all this I will see dreams, see myself fixed in place on the land, hear stories my father taught me.

Late Summer and Fall 1866

Late summer and fall were other seasons of change. Unlike spring, when the land is in a state of flux, late summer is the season when the air above the land changes. The weather rides over the land and for an instant brings relief to our sunburned backs, our aches from the heat, and our parched throats. The weather is mild and cool for an instant. The days grow shorter. The sunsets are more radiant, the mountains turn a brighter purple and red-orange when the sun begins to set. There are breezes and the dust of summer subsides from the air we breathe. The air grows moist at night. There is more dew at morning when we wake. The hint of water returning to a dry land, to the dry smooth stones in the creek. The clouds pass over our heads all day long in a steady parade of shade and light.

Then, as the days move from summer into fall, the clouds build up instead of passing overhead, build up against the mountain peaks that surround us, and the air grows heavy. Then we have thunderstorms in the afternoon, sometimes lingering into early evening, but it is relief to us, this short rain, it cools us, ends the long season of dust and heat. But it is a warning of winter. And we look ahead, all of us, down the long Sierra canyon to see where we'll be when winter hits us; we look until the sun moves lower in the sky and its rays wash the valley with light. Birds escape easily out of the canyon, flying south. Hairy beasts search for food in preparation for their long sleep. The movement of the land comes to a stop. Only the sky moves overhead, scraping the peaks in the afternoons. The sun is low to the ground. The days are shorter. We look again down the valley. There's no way home without walking out of the mountains. The train stays with us. Its soot clouds the sky.

Winter 1867

I spent a winter working on the summit tunnel. Stopped at the summit by more granite and another winter, we had to move trains, rails, tools overland, over the summit, and begin work on the other side while some of us labored at the tunnel. In 1867, the summit tunnel at Donner went into its second winter. I remember every day of winter.

The wind burns my face, throwing hot coals of ice against my skin, the ice wind that strips bark off trees. The white blurs my sight, absorbs all sound around me. I can barely hear my friends talking to me, my ears ache when they do. At night we fear the snowdrifts that cover us up while we sleep. The snow builds up in winter until we climb higher and higher on it, away from the earth that we labor at, carve at, beat our fists against, an immovable granite wall. So that winter we dug out a snow cave that led to the dark summit tunnel. We ate, slept, worked in that ice corridor out of reach of the sharp talons of the wind, but the cold still penetrates us all season long. Outside, needing firewood, we top trees sticking above the snow. The wind butchers my flesh, makes my whole body a wound, and my body's heat rushes to my face and hands to fight back the numbness, but only succeeds in melting the snow that is blowing into my face, and the water is turned to ice. The wet penetrates my skin, my entire body, like pins and every step requires so much effort I hold my breath, tighten my muscles and lift one leg forward, take a breath, and follow with the other leg.

The avalanche is a natural process, a natural occurrence in winter, just as a forest fire was a natural process before man ever stood up and walked around. The fire burned for days, weeks, months down to the edge of the lake, ocean, or desert. It cleansed the earth, and spring still arrived, and began working out of the fine ash. And when the snow gets too heavy for the mountain to hold, it breaks loose. Unlike the granite, the snow's sound shakes the ground, thunders down the trunks of trees, into the ground. Then the whole canyon is filled with its sound as it rips firmly rooted trees out of the earth, breaking others at their exposed tops, grabbing hold of boulders as large as railroad cars to race with them down the canyon walls, the whole slope transforms its expression into a watch until the mass hits the canyon bottom, shaking the frozen roots of trees, the fine bones of pre-historic beasts, lost ocean life. Then the whole canyon shifts into a fall, making rubble of its whiteness.

My strength, our strength combined, is nothing against this season. It is a selfish season. Each of us fights individually against the cold, working harder at night than during the day to fight off the cold of sleep. Each night I lie down exhausted, beaten, defeated, my hands and fingers numb and bleeding from moving cold granite, and the cold wetness covers my body and penetrates my bones as I fall uneasily into sleep. The last energies of the day we save for the night, for a restless sleep. And in the middle of winter, deep in the summit tunnel when the season is at its coldest and stormiest, we work at night and sleep during the day to keep from dying at night in our sleep. So for a few hours during the day, if the sun is out, we go outside and sleep soundly in the sun's brief warm light, baring our wounds to the warmth.

Winter is a season crueler than the men we worked for. All our energies are directed against the winter and to staying alive to greet the first thaw and perhaps the end of the railroad line. And finally, when the railroad is finished, I do not want the seasons to run over my back, letting the days and nights, the weather ride me, break me. I will find a piece of land to work where I can remain in one place and watch the seasons ease on that place, root down in this difficult soil, and nurture my land.

I want to give all the moments of my life the names of places I have been to before, categorize them so that I can lift them out of my memory, find the steady pulse of my life. Root down my life into the names of places. When I'm on the road at night I dream of places I've never been to before, I found places where my dreams joined like arteries out of the heart thick with blood, where my heart pulls at my breath.

CHAPTER TWO

THE NIGHT TRAIN STOPPED AT THE EDGE OF THE OCEAN, THE engine steaming into the waves that lapped against the iron wheels. The ocean was humbled in front of the great steaming engine, its great noise was iron; the moonlight on the ocean gave the sea its place, made the water look like waves of rippling steel. There was a low mumble heard beneath the sound of the waves whose constant voice muted itself against the fine sand; the voices of the men came toward me. I could not see their faces smeared with soot, charcoal faces. Their voices moved past me, toward the ocean, yet I was not afraid, I knew them. They had worked all day on the railroad, but at night they built the great iron engine that brought them to the sea's edge, pointed them home, the way west. They climbed down from the engine, faces black with soot, disguised, to dive into the ocean and swim home, but the moonlight hit the waves and made the surf like bones, white in their faces. Their swimming was useless, their strokes made in a desert of broken bones, of bone hitting bone, hollow noises to men who believed in home and hollow noises to men whose black faces held in their souls. But the engine waited in the iron night. And by morning the sun came up like the hot pulsating engine, the earth steams dry as I walk and kneel and wash my face with the earth's breathing, and the Chinamen all rise around me, their faces clean and grim, rising like swiftly rising steam to walk farther into their forest.

They go back to work, their eyes red with sea salt, their hands red from swimming with the broken bone sea. The black from the iron rails comes off in their hands.

I run through a thick night, that night of black soot mixing with my sweat to drip like tears from my face; my heart is the engine's red iron and if I stop running I will be burned. Now the night driver is me. The old night train filled with Chinamen, my grandfathers, fathers, all without lovers, without women, struggling against black iron with hands splintered from coarse cross ties. I am driving my car, moving out of a narrow side road at ninety onto a highway. With my father's spirit I am driving at night. No music. No more dreams. There is only the blur of the white line, the white guard rail at the edges of my sight as I outrun the yellow glare of lights, an ache at the temples and a pulse in the whites of my palms, knowing what is in front of me. I am speaking to the road with the green lights of the car's instruments touching my face, no dreams, just talk, like an ocean's talk, constant, muted against sand, immediate, suffocating. My fingers moving from the steering wheel, through glass, to grab at the blurs of white at one hundred miles an hour. My hands lift me out of my seat to stoop over and grab at the bleached bones of the road. I reach out to take the road in my hands, the blur of bones, no blood, someone speaks and I do not recognize the voice. Piano music rising in my ears like the winds that move across the plains and sweep like rivers, its waves of voice nearing my ear. The memorized picture fades and I am again speaking to myself with my lovers there, mother and father, and I remind myself what I call them. They begin to move. I give her all my weight, my father gives me his hand to hold saying, "We have to run, hold on." And I hold on for the chase, flying, my feet touching ground every six feet, like giants marching over the earth, my father, the track star, the runner giving me all the soul of his life.

I was never old enough to write a letter to my father to tell him how he had shaped my life. So on a night like this I write him a letter. Standing there on the beach, the night train easing up to me, the engine blacker than the night, is blowing steam out to sea. So I write. Dear Father, I am now at home. At our home on the range, our place. It is April. Tonight I remember a humid night on Guam when I held your forehead in my small hands as I rode on your shoulders. My hands felt your ears, the shape of your chin, and the shape of your nose until you became annoyed and placed my hands back on your forehead and shifted my weight on your shoulders. Like a blind man, I remember your face in the darkness. I remember you now with urgency. In this night here I heard the same sounds of a tropical night; the clicking of insects, the scrape of a lizard's claws on the screen door. Because I am now the same age as you are, Father, I remember how you showed me the buttonholes and buttons of my clothes, the loops needed to tie my shoes. I do not remember whether you admired me then, or remarked to yourself how much I looked like you, or felt satisfied that I would grow into the athlete you were. Tonight I took a long look into your face and saw you smiling. You are twenty-eight years old. At fifteen, when my mother died, I thought my terror would increase with age. The terror that I would not be like you, the terror that I would never admit where my home stood rooted. A woman I love, Father, told me that identity is a word full of the home. Identity is a word that whispers, not whispers, but *gets* you to say, "ever, ever yours."

The night train is beside me, spewing steam. I hear iron gates and doors opening and closing, I feel the heat of the engine beside me. The cold ocean waves boil against the hot iron beneath the engine. The waves wet my shoes and my pants at the ankles. The train fills the whole night. It is a wall between the dry beach and the edge of the ocean. Under the legend of this train, the heart of this country lies in immovable granite mountains, and lies in the roots of giant trees. Those roots are sharp talons in the earth of my country. I stand my ground and wave the train on. The train inches by me, heaving up steam, heat, sand, and seawater. The last thing I remember doing tonight is raising my hand to signal the train on. I walk back to the dock where I am making my stand in the night and see the train gather speed, feel it brush by me. I count every car pulled by the engine until all the noise of the night is gone.

Now I have the loneliness of fathers. To work from my soul, the heart speaking and pledging a feeling and commitment that gives like my father's giving to his lover, my mother. Not in self-pity, since the dream of Great-Grandfather, whose crying left scars on his face, Dear Father, I say, I write, I sing, I give you my love, this is a letter whispering those words, "ever, ever yours." But you are dead. There is nothing that keeps me, no voice, except that voice plagued by memory and objects of no value, a watch, a ring, a sweater, no movement, "keep it close to the skin," I say to myself. Father, I have dreams of departures, people leaving me, of life losing ground. I cannot control the blood that rushes to my head in the night and makes my dreams red.

I am driving at night and the whine of the car's engine rips through second and third gears. The straight road at last, that familiar white blur. A shift at a hundred and ten, deafening my ears. No sound now except for the building whine of my engine, my knees go weak, no blood there. I am too busy for fear, checking oil, rpms, engine heat, speed at a glance, hands and arms working at the wheel, correcting for wind gusts.

I am pointing the car's sloping blue nose at a hundred into the blur of moons. What my eye sees becomes a scream, the scream of moonlight. I take my hands off the road, out of the ocean of bones, my sight returns to that yellow glare of headlights, the car slows to a stop, trembling like the blood at my knees. I move across America picking up ghosts.

My father, the engineer, wrote a love story that he kept with his letters. It was written two years before my birth and only a few weeks after my mother and father were married. He was a serious young man of thirty when he wrote it. It's written in engineer's English.

The Great Waltz

"Everything seems to be all right. What time is it, dear?" she asked. There was no reply. She started to whistle "The Tale of the Vienna Woods" without waiting for an answer. She was busy cooking in the kitchen.

"Boy! What a woman!" he said. She was startled by his answer. She turned around to find out what was wrong with him. He was sitting at ease in the kitchen by the window, his feet up on a chair, and he was eating cookies and candies, concentrating his attention on *Film Fun* magazine.

"What are you looking at? Let me see. You haven't

answered my question yet." She looked over his shoulder at the pictures in *Film Fun* but it was not an interesting picture for a woman.

It was early September in 1947. The newly married couple lived in a small flat in Berkeley, just fifteen minutes from downtown.

Tonight, they were expecting their friends, Jessie, Joan, Norma, and her fiancé for dinner. She was busy all day, decorating the windows with new curtains she had painted herself. She moved the chairs and sofa so that everyone could sit close to each other. She polished the brass teapot. She pushed her piano back toward the stand lamp to make the room more cozy. She put a black stone that looked like a man on the mantel of the fireplace. She liked it very much, but her husband said it was silly to put it on the fireplace mantel, because the fireplace was the center of activity. Both of them wanted to decorate it with their favorite piece.

Since he was an engineer, she let him fix the lamps in the living room so that the light would reflect off the ceiling and walls. The bulbs were properly sheltered, the illumination was moderate.

"Darling, go take a bath before they come. Wash your fingernails carefully. I don't mind if you use some of my 'Soir de Paris.' I just don't want the smell of gasoline in the room tonight."

He was a successful engineer and he liked his job. Every day he drove his car to his office and came back home at 5:30 after a day's hard work. He always came home with a dirty face and hands and oil stains on his clothes. After work he usually sank down into the sofa with his work clothes on. He would listen to the radio and eat a piece of pie. Tonight, the air in the room was tingling with the smell of gasoline and perfume. She did not like his gasoline, but he liked her perfume.

After their dinner, and everyone was relaxing in the living room eating dessert, he said to her, "Let me have a piece of your cake if you don't want anymore." His large figure must have had a large stomach because his appetite was awfully fine. He knew that his guests would not laugh at him for asking for an extra share, because they were old classmates. They had all grown up now, but they never forgot those happy days of school life. When they got together, they laughed and talked just like the old days. Every Saturday or on holidays, they got together. They talked about the past, their hopes, the happy events, and sometimes they danced if the music on the radio was especially fine. They were young and their lives seemed like flowers in May.

"You have completely changed," Jessie said to the hostess, sitting before the piano.

"Yes, she has, just look at the hair, lips, eyelashes, especially the figure. Marriage is good for you," Joan said.

Jessie danced her fingers over the keys. Norma said to Jessie, "Play something."

"Oh no, let our hostess play something! After all it's her piano and she is going to have a concert next Sunday night," Jessie said in a loud voice.

The newly married couple eyed each other for a moment and then she sat down at the piano and began to play selections from "The Great Waltz." It was a happy tune and he sank back down into the sofa with his pipe in his hand. The curling smoke made his mind swim in reveries. He remembered when he first took his bride out. They went ice skating. Her beauty and charm thrilled him. He remembered calling on her with her permission. It was just before he was to leave on a special job and he asked her whether he could have a date with her the next Sunday before he said goodbye. Her answer was not favorable. Time got fast when they were together.

In the late nights of spring, 1957, my mother drove home from Oak Knoll Naval Hospital, thrashing the night traffic, pushing the little car through its gears, and somehow returned home away from the sleepless daze and the edge of crash. She came home joking about amazing dog stories, traveling across the desert, oceans, freezing mountains all in the night without food. Her driving at night seemed to her like swimming the currents of a flooded street, her eyes unfocused on the black night, and still seeing the white hospital bed, father's pale skin and the light in the hospital's solarium that signaled his dying.

And one night she came home early, not joking, not ready to gather me up in her arms to play. She asked what color I wanted my room painted. And in her blank expression I knew that father had died. I started crying. She became angry, not looking at me, and started calling out colors.

My mother taught me how to iron clothes that night. She had a basket full of clothes that had been around for years. The basket never grew or decreased in size. She ironed only what we needed. So when I was seven she told me to iron the back of the collar on my shirt so that the collar won't show wrinkles on the top part that shows. Next, to iron the shoulder area. Then the sleeves. The flap that the buttons are sewn to. Then the left front, the back, and the right front. Hang it up and button the top two buttons. A family tradition had been passed on to me. I don't remember how long I was ironing that night but I ironed all my own shirts. When I had finished ironing my shirts I noticed she had fallen asleep on the couch. I could see her from the kitchen. That was when I started ironing my father's shirts. Most of them were at the bottom of the basket. My father used to send his shirts out to be cleaned and ironed. He would let me put on his huge shirt before he put it on so that I could hear the sound of my hand working its way down the sleeve with that tearing sound because the starch had glued the sleeves shut. He had shirt pockets that held both my hands. I didn't have any starch that night so I ironed his shirts like mine. I folded them all neatly on the kitchen table. Ten white shirts, five light blue shirts, two khaki work shirts, two plaid ones. I reached down into the basket and found myself a set of flannel pajamas. I ironed them and put them on. I took the blanket off my bed and squeezed into a small space next to my mother on the couch and fell asleep with her. The blanket trapped the smells of clean and warm cotton with her perfume and her warm breath.

I had said before that I am violent, that I had become a father to myself. But it was my mother that controlled my growing until she too died eight years after my father's death. Not a startling revelation except when I saw her burial and I discovered that she had shaped the style of my manhood in accordance with her own competitive and ambitious self. I grew up watching my mother's face for direction, the movements of her body. The features of her face shaped me. She was thirty-two years old when my father died and I was seven, and when I think of her now I remember her as a young woman and how her growing kept pace with mine. She would not let me be present at my father's funeral, she did not want to be the object of everyone's pity, the mother of a fatherless child, and she did not want my childhood shaped around the ceremony and ritual of a funeral. And now, after I had witnessed her dying in another hospital eight years later and became the prominent figure at her funeral, I did not cry. I did not want everyone's pity for an orphaned fifteen-year-old boy, but kept my eyes on the casket, kept my hands in my pockets and walked quickly through the ceremony of her death.

After she died I was no longer anyone's son. By my mother's arrangement I was to go off and live with my uncle and aunt until I was eighteen, then I could decide for myself what I wanted to do with my life. They lived along the California coast by a large lagoon. My uncle kept my mother's old Volkswagen there until I turned sixteen and learned how to drive. I suffered from dreams in that car. I remembered a lot of life driving around in my mother's car.

After my father's death, my mother took me to Carmel on weekends and only there, while I played on the beach and she walked along the ocean's edge, did she show her despair. I knew she brought me to the white sandy beaches of Carmel because it reminded her of our last happy days as a family on Guam. She merely wished that I should continue my uninterrupted childhood from one beach to another. But I had already lost my role as a child at the age of seven when I noticed her desperate efforts and private despair. A child doesn't accept tragedy in the same light as an adult because in the fantasy world of the hero in books and movies the hero has no weaknesses other than his own mortality, and sometimes even that is questionable. So out of my vacated childhood I wanted to show my mother that I had accepted Father's death and needed her real life around me. I inherited a melodramatic strength, a hero's arrogance, I was able

34

to take care of myself, and her death further entrenched that strength. I grew up out of the ruins of a childhood, yet the fantasies and myths a child believes in fathered me through those years. When I entered high school, I entered with a stoic, not passive, acceptance of the stereotyped insane adolescent years. Whether I had known or not, I had grown beyond those years and the social life of a teenager was a blank. There were no dates, no dances, just swimming miles and miles and playing water polo. I was a poor student because that role did not fit into the concept of myself, but the direct test of my physical abilities did.

A few years after my father died, my mother opened a flower shop. She taught me the flower business until I was able to assist her and prepare the flowers for weddings, assemble corsages, and make flower arrangements for all occasions. When customers wanted something "exotic," like one of those "Japanese modernistic" flower arrangements, my mother would smile and take their order and charge them appropriately for a custom-made, one-of-a-kind arrangement dug out of our supposed misty Oriental heritage. She always let me make those floral arrangements, and I worked like a demented Dr. Frankenstein in his laboratory, twisting ti leaves into circles, shredding leaves into fountains of green splinters amid pieces of wood and stone, and arranging three lone but strategically placed flowers known by all to symbolize sun, man, and earth. The customers were always pleased by the work of art, never knowing that a fourteen-year-old kid wearing a letterman's jacket, jeans, and black tennis shoes was behind the creation.

Three mornings a week she had sent me with the driver to the flower market, and to me it had been the fulfillment of the childish gesture of bringing flowers home to mother. Except I brought home several hundred of the finest hothouse-grown flowers. And it was on those mornings that I felt vibrant and alive, stepping into the warehouse where the growers set up tables, piled high with flowers. The air was so thick with flowers that it soaked into my clothes and stayed with me for hours afterward. After she died, it was that thick sweet smell of the flower market that froze me on the edge of shock, made me sick to my stomach. That same smell followed my mother when she came out with the flowers from the storage refrigerator into the dusty smells of the warm storefront. Holidays for everyone else became hectic labor all night long for us. Mother's Day was always the worst. We boxed roses and made corsages all night long until we finished the day's orders. And at the end of all this we would go home without a single flower for my own mother, and she would always say, when I pointed out the lack of flowers in our own home, "We spend more time at the shop and that's where the flowers are. Besides, I've told you that 'the cobbler's son has no shoes.'"

In the evening following her funeral I stood in the darkened store, silent except for the refrigerator fans cooling the flowers. I did not cry at her funeral, and now standing in the tomb of her energies I wanted to cry for my loss, but with almost no sleep in the three days following her death I simply felt a moment of relief away from the relatives and friends. I walked up to the display refrigerator and opened the door to turn off the fluorescent lights. The cold sweet air pushed out at me and I started to get sick, I shut off the fans of the refrigerator but the air still filtered out as I backed away from the opened door.

My mother had brought me beyond those years. I lost myself, my role as a student, and could not grasp anything that was not relevant to my sense of tragedy, except competition. The need to compete filled my life, especially when my mother was dying and slipping from my grip. I brought to her bedside my water polo awards, the swimming medals. But she saw that I was now like my father, the track star, the basketball and ice hockey player, and whether I had realized it then or not did not matter to her, she had succeeded in forming me into her notion of manly style, and in her eyes I had become simply her husband's son. She must have seen the hints of his sensibility in my personality and their own conspicuously romantic past, because in the middle of a perfect recovery, she died in the night.

After my mother died, I never wanted to be alone. I was in competition with everyone except myself. I was driving at night. I was driving with my father. When I was three, he had decided it was time he and his family saw America. He drove a brown, clattering, stubborn Hillman Minx across the country and back, across the plains of America, into big cities like Chicago and New York. I slept most of the way and only remember a day in New York, a day in Washington, D.C., at the Lincoln Memorial, a store in Oklahoma where he bought me a slingshot, and I remember standing at the rim of the Grand Canyon. And when we came home, he never spoke of that journey again while I was growing up except to say that "we had done it."

Until my father died he had brought me up on all the childhood heroes. He indulged me in my fantasies and fascinations with planes, cars, cowboys, comic book heroes, and trains. He took me down to Berkeley's Aquatic Park two or three times a week to watch the trains pull in to the factories bordering the lake. We sat in the car parked under a tree watching the trains for hours at a time. My father sat in the back seat of the car and napped, smoked, and read the newspaper while I stood up on the front seat watching for trains. My father always read every page of the paper, beginning with the first page and ending on the last page of the financial section. If stories were continued on other pages, he wouldn't turn to them until he had read all the stories in between. He read the paper as people do riding on a crowded bus, folding it lengthwise and reading half of the paper at a time instead of holding it at arm's length.

The boxcars were too far away for me to read the names on the sides, so while they were pulling in or pulling out I called out the names of the states and big cities I knew. I always called the caboose "Berkeley," for our hometown. And after a while if I saw that a train was leaving, I'd wake my father up and make him rush to a crossing gate so that I could see, up close, the sides of the cars, listen to them building up speed, hear the rhythm of the iron wheels keeping time with the ringing bell at the crossing gate in front of us.

On Guam, the bombers at the Air Force base took the place of the trains. My father and I would stand at the end of the runway as I plugged my ears, clenched my teeth, wrinkled my face into what must have looked like an expression of great pain, as the bombers thundered off the runway about a hundred feet over us, shaking the ground and blowing two-hundred-mile-an-hour dust at us.

I remember those bombers like friends. My father took pictures of them for the family album. The B-47s made a lot of noise with their jet engines, and I always liked to see them land and their chutes pop out of their tails. But there was no real detail to the B-47s; they were sleek, fast, and efficient-looking. There were no names on the B-47s like "Rosie" or "Betty Sue," just numbers. The old B-29s were turned into weather planes and their tails were painted orange. Before the B-47s came to Guam, the base was filled with a kid's closest friend—the B-36. It looked like a giant toothpick, with a bubble cockpit up front, a straight back tail, and swept wings. It killed the enemy by making them laugh. It looked like a silver boat with six outboard engines on the rear of the wings. It was like a kid's drawing of fancy planes, except this one flew.

And when my father took pictures of those planes for me, and when we waited hours for those trains to pass by Aquatic Park, he encouraged my enthusiasm and imagination. At night, when the trains were no longer visible, he drove me down to Emeryville to see the enormous "Sherwin Williams Paints Cover the Earth" neon sign, watching the red lights pour down over the earth out of the giant, green-lighted paint can. He walked with me. He towed me up and down the sidewalks in a red wagon. He kept pace with my youth. He was Bobby to me. And when he died, my mother knew she had to tell me about his youth and the lives of my grandfathers as he had told her. She had to tell me who kept pace with his youth, what was the grief that shaped his sensibility, and who struggled to make a place for him, for me. She had to make me more than just her husband's son, more than understanding his sensibility, but rather make me realize it on my own and sometime in my life say simply that "I am the son of my father."

When the nurse dropped my mother's thick green jade bracelet into my hands, the circle of green stone moved in my hands, turned red. I could not let go of it. It was the sound of her heart. She has no shape for me now, only my echo, and she kept my youth like cool green jade. She had a lower two years after my father died who moved like a ghost around my mother, loving her like artificial heat, dry, stifling, a silent heat that kept me secret in my play. No heroes, only that dark love, that dry heated love, the smell of exhaust and warmed car heat, stifling my breath for some air outside the windows. I stayed cool by put-ting my ear to the window and listening to the highway air, my cheek pressed against the glass. It felt like ice in the windy forest of friends, my heroes climbing, fighting, shooting, running alongside the car, waving frantically, calling me into the forest to join their gang, ride their train, and I forgot the ceaseless hum of the car's heater. I was running on iron wheels, my face in the wind, breathing frozen air and white engine steam, the fear of my mother's love toward him moved me and made me run in my dreams, pointless, frantic, running nowhere, just to run and feel my own secret and the pain of breath. It is only when I wake that I am frightened, feeling that somehow I have progressed, leaving myself behind at the same time. I am violent. I give myself names to prove the fantasy, but the dream eludes me.

She thought that now the nights of crying could be solved by this new love. Yet her grief was still overpowering her; she held on to her grief for her dead husband and lover, crying at nights, taking her well-kept grief out of its hiding place to cry herself to sleep. I would hear her moaning and crying. Only in the first days after my father's death did I cry silently into my pillow, my lover, my hero gone, his name whispered on my lips as I cried; then one day I stopped crying for him, resolved to make my life like his; it gave me strength. And it was my resolve not to cry anymore that always drove me to my mother to comfort her in her grief. Her grief became my duty. I watched her tears fall to the pillow, asking her not to cry, impatient, knowing that all her strength was leaving her, and somehow I thought if I put my mouth to the tear-stained pillow and sucked the tears from the white case, her energy would pass to me in the warm salt of those tears. And when she died I was mad that she had failed me. She had no longer wanted to stand by my side. After my mother died I was alone, but I did not cry. My sleep tore me apart, and gave her flesh back to me in pieces, her voice with no substance, and finally nothing but a hollow sound would wake me, her jade bracelet knocking against the house as she moved around, cleaning, cooking, writing. It had become for me, in those dreams, the rhythmic beating of her heart. There was no need for me to put my head against her chest to hear the beating of her heart. The cold stone, jade in my eyes, filled my youth and kept time with the unsteady beating of my own heart.

CHAPTER THREE

I

I CAME TO LIVE WITH MY UNCLE AND AUNT AT THE AGE OF fifteen in a small town near the ocean in California, I came to them as a son. Not their son, just a son. I came to them on an overcast day, when the ocean fog moved through eucalyptus leaves, making them drip with moisture, making the leaves so heavy they fell to the road. The moisture splattered against my uncle's car as we drove home.

My uncle is the husband of my mother's sister. He is a physician and I presumed loved my aunt because in the three years I lived with them they provided a quiet and happy life for me. My uncle is also a bad driver. Doctors are supposed to be good with their hands, good with tools and useful instruments. I noticed that he was an absentminded driver. Perhaps he was nervous the day he brought me home to live with him and my aunt, but that day his feet didn't seem to know what his hands and eyes were doing. He braked too soon on corners, braked too late, lugged the engine in high gear, and generally forgot, what gear he was driving in, because from time to time he would reach for the gear-shift knob and not find it until he looked down. He was talkative that day, perhaps because he was ill at ease, for I learned later that he usually did not carry on a conversation merely for the sake of conversation. He never imposed his ego on me to try and make me into something, his son, an educated man, a thrifty person, anything. He simply provided for me and assumed the responsibility of a parent. He gave me whatever I needed. He gave little advice except when I asked for it. He never scolded me, and I don't think I ever needed scolding while I lived with him. I respected him and what he was. He respected my private grief. Or what he must have thought was grief or tragedy. We were polite.

"Rainsford, I think you'll like living out near the ocean. It's quiet. It's a small town. It has been quite cold out here lately. They said it was snowing out at sea the other day." He braked hard for a corner and then drifted through it, stepped on the gas and let the car lurch for a moment. I heard the clutch slipping. He downshifted.

My uncle is average in height and weight. His hairline is receding, which he jokes about from time to time. He is a good doctor. He works hard. He enjoys his private life. He even jogs on the beach in the mornings. My uncle and aunt have no children. I am sure he came to feel at ease with me because he didn't have to make an effort to raise me. I sometimes jogged with him on the beach. He is a sincere man. He never uses clichés to express himself. He is a precise man.

When my uncle and aunt came to pick me up, I met him at the door and shook his hand and corrected my posture. "How are you, Uncle?" My aunt, behind him, was wiping her tears away from her cheeks. Things were beginning to come back to me in a logical order. Everything I did after my mother's death reminded me of something we had done together. As I grasped my uncle's hand I was thinking about the time I was eating a hamburger in the back room of the flower shop.

"Shake my hand," my mother said.

"Huh?"

"Shake my hand."

"What for?" I asked as I spoke through a mouthful of hamburger. This was the mother I wanted to kiss like the movie stars when I was a little boy after seeing those movies of the stars grabbing each other, smearing lipstick, mussing up each other's hair, and gasping for breath. "Kiss me like in the movies, Mom," I said then in the dark of my room as she came to tuck me in.

She laughed, "Like what?"

"Kiss me like in the movies, Mom."

She laughed again and bent down close to kiss me goodnight.

"Close your eyes," I said. She closed her eyes. We kissed. In the dark. My room. "Goodbye," I said from the throat.

"Goodbye. Goodbye," she said, backing out and closing the door.

"Don't close the door all the way."

Now she was saying shake my hand. I pretended to be serious as she was. "Mother . . . this . . . isn't . . . goodbye, is it?"

"Just come over here and shake my hand."

I looked in her hand to see if there was a buzzer in it, then shook her hand safely. "How do you do?" I said.

"Shake it again." I shook. "Harder." I shook harder. "Harder." I shook her hand as firmly as I could. "Now," she said, "whenever you are introduced to another man, remember to shake his hand as firmly as you can. End of lesson."

I was shaking my uncle's hand firmly and looking him straight in the eye. "I'm ready to go."

After my father's death it was easy to be my father's son. After my mother's death it was no longer easy to be just a son. It was no longer easy to be anyone's son. Their deaths forced me to be a grown man at fifteen. At the time of my mother's death, my heart and soul grew into what I thought was worldly. I became the man my uncle was. I picked up his habits. I dressed like him. He wore practical, useful, and long-lasting clothes. Except for his suits, he usually wore corduroy hiking pants, wool sweaters with leather patches on the elbows, wool or corduroy jackets, and plaid flannel shirts.

My aunt was somewhat like my mother, except her responsibility for me sometimes got the best of her and I became her duty. She was my mother's older sister. She went out of her way to give me the best. She was enthusiastic about my future. She wanted me to make plans. She spoke at length to my uncle about me, about what they should do to help me, and he just said to her to let me rest and take it easy. He knew that the death of my parents would give me ambition enough. He didn't even advise me to finish high school if I didn't want to. He left everything up to me. At first, when I started college, I wanted to be a doctor. I wanted to find the secret of things, to *learn*. But in the end, all those courses in chemistry and biology didn't express the flux of my life. They weren't my own voice.

My aunt often said more than she had to say. On that first day driving to their home, she turned around to face me in the rear seat of the car, putting her arm around the back of the front seat.

"You just let us know anything you need. You know, within reason, I mean we can't get you a sailboat or an airplane." She laughed, then brushed a curl from her forehead—she always did that when she changed subjects or moods. My uncle told me that.

"I know what you must be going through and everything. It must have been a terrible thing when your father died and now this. I mean, Rainsford, we'll try to make a nice home for you. There's a good high school not far away. The people around here are nice people. We enjoy being out here by the ocean."

"I understand and appreciate everything you've done. I don't want you to go out of your way."

"Oh, we don't need any thanks or anything like that. I mean, just between you and me, I think you're mature enough, a young man and everything. Your mother often made me promise to watch out for you if anything happened to her after your father died. You've grown into such a mature young man, I'm sure you can take care of yourself, but we'll be right there if you need anything at all." She looked away for a second at her husband, who looked in the rearview mirror at me. She brushed the same curl from her forehead. "I know nothing can take the place of your mother and father, but I want you to know that we'll treat you like our own son." She turned back to face the road, blew her nose, and probably wiped a tear from her eye. I was tired and the sound of the tires on the wet pavement put me to sleep until we arrived at their house. She is a good woman and she tried hard to be a mother to a grown man of fifteen.

When I began to live with them I realized that was the beginning of my private life. They gave that to me. And that private life of my own was what kept me out of touch socially with the other students. I remember those three years with my aunt and uncle as a period of isolation. It was a time when I tested myself in private occupations like jogging on the beach, surf fishing, and competing on the swimming team. I made friends with my uncle. I made his life more physically active.

Certain habits like what I ate, my manners, my routine, and

how I dressed only supplied the façade to my manhood at fifteen. There are no causes, no serious love affairs with a woman, no real independence at fifteen. I was looking for something meaningful while I lived with my aunt and uncle and while I attended high school. At fifteen you are more selfish than at any other age. I wanted a lot of things, but I was, at my uncle's house, in a state of stagnation. I was content and independent at the same time, which only made me more ambitious. I do not recall anything specific about school except I felt the need to be creative and to compete. Two needs that conflict with the state of being content.

Sometimes we would jog on the beach together. On a leisurely jog one sunny day we paused for a short rest. My uncle sat down on a log facing the ocean while I sat on the warm sand and looked out to sea.

"You know," my uncle said, "your grandfather was the first member of the family to come out here."

"You mean right here?" I let some sand run through my fingers and looked back at my uncle.

"When he was a boy he came up to work on some of the ranches. He also worked on a road gang building a road from the east side of the country to here." My uncle picked up some smooth stones and rolled them around in his hand. "As the story goes, he wanted to be a *vaquero*. Some of the Chinese were expert horsemen and many of the ranchers couldn't afford not to let them ride. Your grandfather taught himself how to ride a horse. If he had some free time and he had gotten to know one of the ranch hands, he would get them to lend him their horse. Sometimes they would give him a wild horse and laugh at him getting thrown off." He laughed and tossed one of the stones out to sea. I turned to watch it sail over the waves. He continued, "But after a while they respected him for his perseverance and gave him good horses. They even taught him some rope tricks. I guess they were amused with the idea of a Chinese *vaquero*."

"How did you find out about these stories?"

"I don't really remember. I think it was a lady that used to live with your grandmother over in Oakland. I think when they were married and living in Oakland, he used to take care of some of the horses over there. Anyway, you know how old people talk."

I lay back in the sun and closed my eyes to the bright sun. There was a slight breeze coming in off the ocean. I tried to imagine my grandfather riding along the beach here. My uncle spoke up again, letting out a big yawn, "You know the ranchers used to have big parties down here on the beach, big feasts. If your grandfather ever worked for those ranchers he probably would have been down here helping out with the party. The Chinese who worked for private ranches like that usually did a variety of jobs."

I never kept a diary. Those words were useless. I chose the land around me, my grandfather's America, to give me some meaning and place here, to build something around me, to establish my tradition. I wanted to know exactly what I had left. I wrote a passionately and philosophically vague and abstract paper in my English class which embarrassed me in front of the class but it gave some direction and began to root something deep behind my façade. I called it "Heritage Is a Lonely Place."

Heritage Is a Lonely Place

Out here by the sea where I live the land is drab. No lush greens dominate the land. There are the brown-scented figures of the eucalyptus trees, the thick dune grasses, the wild brush, the occasional dull purple of thistle or the soiled white of Queen Anne's Lace, and the disarrayed forms of the junipers. There is a wildness in the singular colors of this land because of the ocean's spirit, the ocean's voice, the ocean's smell. Without the ocean, this strip of land would not exist as it does. It would seem just another town in America. But it is the whole dramatic coast that sweeps south on jagged cliffs that makes it. In the night when the first winter storms pass over this point, raging, dragging the winds and the rains across the land, the thunder is the waves crashing at my doorstep. In the morning I look out across the fields before me and see that the grasses have been matted down by more than heavy dew. There is nothing easy about winter out here. The rains rage, at high tide the lagoon floods the lowlands, washes out the road, the mud slides in torrents from around the roots of trees, the roots of homes.

In the calm days, the birds of the country rest here. The Great Blue Heron, white egrets, the brown pelican, the marsh hawk, ducks, California quail, kingfishers, gulls, and an occasional hawk in flight over the hills.

In the calm days after the first winds of winter, when all the summer-dried pine needles and redwood branches have broken and scattered on the ground, the air smells of trees for days. Those smells that soak into my clothes, my hair, are thick smells of the tree sap oozing out of the broken branches, the smells of the wet earth. After the first hard rain, the ocean turns from its summer blue colors to winter muddy browns.

There are redwood trees near here that have been struck by lightning but it is the best wood in the world, and the crack and fire of the storm that tries to burn the giant redwood only smolders beneath the bark, and in the weaker ones the fire chars the tree hollow. And it was here that I told all the stories of four generations of my own life. Out of this pure day where I rose up at sunrise to meet my grandfather's life here, where I felt the presence of his heart against the walls, heard it as noise in the night. I rose up to the dawn to greet the clean scent of dew at my feet. And out of so much responsibility to create the whole vision of my life in America, of our lives in America, their death gave me my own clear voice, gave me the heart speaking, but it was not my own heart to use.

I don't think I really knew what I meant by heart then. It came to me later in a dream I had of my grandfather, who came back to this place. This home by the ocean where I lived for three years. It was a land that I investigated completely with my uncle. We hiked along the coast, into the hills above the ocean, around the lagoon, took notes on the change of wildlife and flowers. This small ocean town was my own isolation, my own contentment. It was the place my grandfathers and my father appeared to me in dreams. The heart is a place.

II

AFTER YOU LEFT THE CITY SEVENTY YEARS AGO, GRANDFATHER, and rode north to log the valley of trees just north of here, I knew I saw you out by this lagoon, my uncle's town, and saw your story pass before my eyes. I've been on the streets of your home in Chinatown, where seventy years ago it cracked and moaned of wood, where in the walls of the night you stood alone with the smells of the street, the dark night, the horses of the street. You sailed out of the bay and into this lagoon. I saw you walk up to the water's edge where the tide left stones and small pieces of driftwood in the meadow grasses of the lagoon. You felt yourself captive in the grasses, watched the rippling waves move slowly toward you, felt the moan of your spirit meeting the shallow waters, felt your spirit meeting the sliding roots of trees. I saw you disappearing in the low rays of the setting sun.

What was it that you saw out on the lagoon, Grandfather? If it was a hot day, and memorable because hot days were few, you saw the day mirrored in the lagoon's waters. By its stillness, you noticed the life of the day, those isolated days of heat. The insects flew close to the surface of the water, and you saw them like waves of heat in the steam of the shallowest parts. The birds stalked fish, the black-legged egrets, the blue herons, their wire-thin legs not even rippling the water when they took a step. The day was humid, as a coast gets without a sea breeze. You heard pine cones popping in the branches of the pine tree above you.

If the day was a cold drizzle of a day, did you see the pelicans splashing out in the middle of the lagoon? Did you see them flying in the eucalyptus winds? And in the rain, did you feel how the coldness of day made you ache? Did you see and smell the leaves of the eucalyptus trees on the road in front of you? Grandfather, did you go down to the beach in the heavy rains to examine the tide pools, expecting to see more? As if you and life along the reef were in one element? The rain dripped down your face into the corners of your eyes, and you tasted the air-fresh rain, smelled the ocean's mist. How many stones did you throw out into the sea when you decided that this was the place for roots?

We dreamed of your grandfather and your father. They came

to us, touching our skin with their clothes, a shirt with no color, a shirt without buttons, it smelling of pines. The clothes of fathers. The city was in my dream now, startling some deer in the timid night. You made yourself visible against the night like a flight of owls. My sight moved across your path, I saw you, I saw the fog move in among the trees, and the leaves of the trees drip with moisture and the fog moves in thicker, the eucalyptus leaves fall wet to the ground. You were laughing in the night, said something in Chinese about Fong's new wife, said that we were invited to tea with them, all the men were going to see her, said her name was Mary. Did you hear that? There was a new woman in Chinatown, and Fong was giving a tea to the men in Chinatown to show off his new bride. Grandfather said, "Let's go and see what we can see." We lit out for Chinatown, leaving the sea behind us.

They said she was beautiful, a woman from the north, educated by missionaries who named her Mary; she could speak English to the men. Fong was a man of vision: he had sent for a woman and people spoke of her even in the street. They said she even had a hoop skirt an Englishwoman had given her as a present before she set out for America. But she came to Fong in silks and served us tea, saying in English each time she gave us a cup of tea, "It is my privilege to meet you, sir." And to my grandfather she said, while all the men looked her way, "Fong informs me that you are second generation. I am very privileged to meet a man who knows of the ways of America."

It was the attention that made you lonely in your youth, Grandfather. We were motherless and wifeless in a town of men, in a country that hated us, and from the day I found you with your face in your hands, seventy years later from that point of your furious youth, you found a woman who fathered my father and he fathered me. And could have said to Mary that night when we were the same age, "This is my grandson. He is fourth generation." We rode on horses through the valleys at the base of Mt. Tamalpais, where in the shadows of the mountainside we huddled against the grazing moonlight. We walked along the beach at sunset, pulling our horses behind us toward home. We camped on the white beach, looking north, at one edge of our lagoon. We looked south along the rocky and jagged cliffs. Our horses fed on the coarse dune grass. And all night we watched the moon set in the waves. You saw the ocean become like a plain in the night.

We were riders out on a plain where the autumn skies put more color in the sandstone hills. Perhaps you were in Wyoming when the nights grew colder, when the thunderstorms moved in in the late afternoon and made the day humid. We rode west on the plains toward this home, this lagoon, where, on the western rise of the mesa, you looked down on the ocean, brought yourself even with the short days, the setting sun. We counted our steps to the west, slept on the shifting plains, as the seasons passed over us. And when the first snows of winter fell on us somewhere near Idaho, we led our horses to safety. I followed your path, looking down at the snowflakes tangled in the branches of the low bush that grew on sands of the plains. The snowflakes were stars entering the path after you.

When you saw the hills of our home, the hills that rise up out of and shape the lagoon, you shouted back to me that the first rains had already fallen here. The first sprouts of the grasses were coming up and the brown earth was turned darker with moisture. I saw your pelicans splashing out in the water. Then they took flight in the wind, moved out west to the seacoast. You followed them, climbing out among the jagged rocks on the beach, and sat where the crashing waves broke at your feet, sending a spray of sea up around you. But you stood your ground and watched the brown pelicans cruise the tops of the waves like ships. Your horse stood by, watching you.

You laughed at the ponderous brown pelicans flying in the wind. And you told me that they come to this area to mate, splashing around the lagoon, showed me how they're shaped like great travelers, the large wing span, how they glide with only a few flaps of their wings, and how they fish in among the ocean swells. Finally, you said great travelers make great lovers. And I laughed.

My own father traveled to Australia and fell in love there with the Englishwoman who made fun of the way he talked. She would assume a deeper voice and imitate his voice to him, "Yep, howdy, sure, good thing, whatya think of that, gimme my coffee black." Yes, Grandfather, good travelers make good lovers.

You watched me as I grew. You saw me at sixteen when my uncle gave me my mother's old 1958 Volkswagen for my own car. I taught myself how to drive. I spent most of my time fixing the car up; cutting up old carpets for the floor and washing and waxing it. When the interior and seats started falling apart, I bought a walnut-grained gear-shift knob to make it look slick. I spent most of my time driving around at night thinking about my life, driving around in the hills looking at night views, driving past places where I used to live, past houses of friends. Then I'd drive home.

This lagoon is colder than the one I knew on that island, Guam, so full of sunsets to color my skin, and winds to cool. This lagoon mixes the smell of eucalyptus and the salt of freezing waves.

I was driving around the lagoon in the thick night fog. I had memorized every turn, every pothole in the road, and even in the semi-drizzle of the fog I drove fast, but as I took each turn at the car's limit, the same curves that froze tourists to their steering wheels and brakes, I saw something else on the road, and only out of habit I took each corner perfectly. I saw the taillights of a white van disappear around the curve in front of me. I stepped on the throttle to pull closer to the van before it disappeared around the next bend and saw that its rear doors were open. There were landmarks I always watched for that signaled turns where I had to brake and downshift to second. One was a milepost just before a rising right-hand corner which banked to the outside. I took the turn easily in second, noticing that the rear wheels had slipped slightly on the fog-wet pavement. My eyes started to ache as I strained to see the van in front of me. Just as I was gaining on it, it seemed to be pulling farther away. I rolled down the window, letting in the ocean air, and turned the corner and just as I thought I was losing ground, I somehow had pulled within three car lengths of the van. The doors were open, flowers were falling out of the open rear doors, and then it disappeared around the next corner. I knew I was dreaming it was our old delivery van. It was a dream I knew well.

I looked out over this meadow when the winds of the ocean rushed through and saw a woman leaning into the wind, her black hair giving lines to the wind, she held her hat on her head with one hand. And I went out to meet her, bring her in from the wind, but she was gone and I was left alone.

I slowed and downshifted for another corner. The road was slick and the car started to slide, but I was still in control when I saw the van broadside, blocking the road in the fog, flowers scattered around it. Yellow, red, and pink flowers interrupted my concentration on the white fog and black night road. Their bright intrusion into the night was like blinding lights to me. I hesitated too long. I braked hard but that only increased the angle of my slide. As the back of the car started to drift to the left, I slid sideways with my headlights flashing on the blurred features of the cliff, and even the van was now to my left and dark. I spun the wheel to the left and headed away from the cliff and in the direction of the lagoon's shore, which borders the road. The van was still blocking the road, and now my lights illuminated the waters and I saw a narrow strip of shoreline between the water and the edge of the road. I pressed down on the accelerator to straighten out and get by the van on the dirt, but I was going too fast and the rocks along the shoreline wrenched the steering wheel from my hands. I heard them flying underneath my wheels against the bottom of the car, and in that instant, when I should have reacted again, I was stopped short of the water by the green stagnant muck of the shore, and I sat in the seat with both hands on the steering wheel, the headlights shining on stagnant waters near land. I heard the driver of the van running down to help me. I heard the squishing sounds of his shoes as he walked carefully in the muck to my side of the car. He opened the door and grabbed me by the elbow and supported me as I turned to get out.

"Are you okay? Watch your step in this mud." He helped me back to the road. As he spoke, I looked at the face of this driver as if I knew him, I let him help me keep my balance.

I stopped to look at my mother's car in the mud. The car seemed unsteady in the mud. I should have known just before she went into the hospital that she was weakening. She demanded more of me when she couldn't do the job herself. She would sit behind the long work table in the back room of the flower shop and tell me what to do, throw orders around, making me hustle from one job to the next, all on the pretense she was teaching me the business.

"After you finish changing the water in the back refrigerator, I want you to box a dozen roses for . . ." She turned around on the high stool and looked up at the board with the week's orders: ". . . uh, Wilson. The card is right here."

She clipped it to the order. I set the heavy can of water I was carrying on the table opposite her.

"It's way past lunch. You ought to get something to eat."

"What you mean is *you* want something to eat," she said.

"I had a snack at home before I came down here. I mean, you ought to eat something."

"I'll wait until dinner."

She glanced up at me and put down the receipts she was looking through and said, "You know that school jacket of yours is way too big for you. You couldn't wait for one your size, could you? You had to put that letter of yours on something right away."

"The store wasn't getting in any jackets for a couple of months."

"Are the girls impressed with your medals and your letter?"

"Yeah, that's why I got it so big. My girlfriend is so big and fat when I lend it to her it'll fit."

"Go empty the water."

"You ought to eat something. A hamburger . . ."

"Wilson is coming in for the roses . . ."

". . . some fries, a milkshake . . ."

". . . in twenty minutes. Are you going to box those roses or will I have to do it?"

"How about a nice milkshake? If you can't finish it, I'll drink the rest."

"What are you—my mother? I didn't raise you to be my mother. You're my slave. Don't bug me."

"I got to take care of my girlfriends. My skinny mother needs milkshakes and my fat girlfriend needs skim milk."

"Okay, empty the water and go down and get a milkshake."

"I'll start the roses when I get back."

". . . and take off that jacket. You look ridiculous. You don't have to impress me."

"Okay. I got some money already. I even got enough for some fries. Chocolate okay?"

"Fine."

I stopped at the door. "Say, why don't we bring some flowers home tonight? You used to do that all the time before we had the shop."

She put down the receipts again and said, "You know it's different now. We have to sell these. You know, the cobbler's son . . ."

"Yeah, no shoes, no shoes."

"Don't say yeah, say yes."

"I'm wearing nine-dollar Converse basketball shoes on my feet. You bring home the flowers and I'll buy the milkshakes."

"Yeah, yeah."

She used to tell my father not to say yeah in front of me. In raising me she was unlike most mothers, who used self-pity to stir their sons into some kind of responsible action. I was like her. Mothers would think of the saddest thing in the world to say to their sons to inspire devotion or fidelity through guilt. For us, the saddest thing in the world had happened already. It was only after her death that I had to strive to be a son. It was after her funeral that I cried because my father had died eight years before her.

From her hospital bed she spoke to me, murmured something about my having the same sense of humor my father had, about how all the girls were after him, about how much of an athlete he was. She asked me to put on my letterman's jacket. I bent

over to kiss her good-night and she clutched the cool white leather sleeves of my jacket.

"The accident was all my fault. I was blocking the road. I hope you're not hurt."

We stepped around to the front of his van and into the headlights. I saw now that he was not the same man who had driven me three mornings a week to the flower market. I let him apologize. The sickening sweet smell of the flowers mixed with the ocean air, and I thought of the night I backed away from the open door of the refrigerator in the flower shop.

I was walking on the cleanly lit streets of downtown Berkeley. The city was deserted, a few cars drove past slowing at the blinking yellow light at the intersection, a bus waited at the corner. Everything about this town is fixed at night, nothing seems temporary, even the newspaper man standing on the corner reading a paperback book in the streetlight seemed fixed. The movie theater was already dark. Some of the store windows were lit. I was looking for one store I knew well, the store where my father had built shelves when he was a student. My aunt had owned the children's store then and it was after we came home from Guam that I spent many weeks there with my aunt while my mother visited my father in the hospital.

I was standing in front of the store that night in Berkeley. It was one of those nights that caused men to revisit old homes, places where they used to roam, places where their childhood was rooted. I was already dreaming of those places that night, places of love. With my hands pressed on the plate-glass window, I peered into the darkened store to see if those shelves were still there. I heard a laugh in the night store. I saw everything as it was. I was sliding on the smooth floor with only my socks on, my arms outspread to balance my flight. I worked for my aunt and she paid me twenty-five cents an hour, plus ice cream from the corner fountain. I swept the floors with that big broom like it was a race car. I played cool to other boys who came into the store with their mothers because I owned the store. I smirked at little girls. And when they went into the dressing room with my aunt and their mothers, I would run upstairs to the storeroom, tiptoe around to a place in the floor directly over the dressing room where a knot in the wood floor had fallen out, and peek down through the floor into the dressing room at little girls, at five layers of petticoats, at the top of mothers' heads. I got dusty up there, pushing old boxes around, punching mannequins my size.

Yes, Grandfather, you watched me as I grew. You knew when I was ten I took my first journey alone, Mother put me on a train to go from Berkeley to Turlock, put me in the car behind the engine, told me to stay put and not to get off until Turlock. And when the train pulled out of the station, she quickly called my uncle and told him I was in the second car, told him to meet the proud traveler at the station. For the first time I passed on the other side of Aquatic Park, where my father had parked to show me the trains. I read the names of the stations we passed, and felt the heat of the Central Valley through the window. I fought sleep all the way.

You were the one Grandfather who told me that all points along a journey should be named. Given the names of the heart. There should be no excuse for the journey. Your simple reason of "let's go and see what we can see" should be reason enough. I was always intrigued with the sight of Mt. Shasta, remembering my father's vision at its base, that dark woman that came to him in the pre-dawn night, and every time I passed that mountain I saw it change. In summer I saw it as a pile of loose talus and scree, with only a few patches of snow. In winter it usually

was obscure and stormy, so white I could hardly make out the ridges, peaks, couloirs, and shadows. In spring, the mountain was in its most inviting state; the days were clear and windy, the glaciers seemed larger; near the top, the winds were blowing snow banners off the peaks and the bare rock of the ridges.

I climbed Shasta a few years ago. You saw me there, followed me in the trudge to Lake Helen, up the snowfield above Lake Helen where the thirty-five-degree snowfield was ice. The wind came down the field, raising granules of ice that pelted a bare spot on my face. You followed me, Grandfather, or perhaps you yourself were there, on the last 2,000 feet to the 14,000–foot summit plateau, pacing with my slow steps, losing me at times in the snow banners flying off the ridges of rock, pacing my steps with yours, past places bearing names like The Heart, The Red Banks, Heartbreak Ridge, Desperation Ridge, and Misery Hill. At times I turned to the south in those last steps to the summit, stamping my crampons into the ice, planting my ice ax, and squatting down to see the view of the valley, where it was sixty degrees warmer. Our backs were to the wind. I turned from the last look to make my way to the summit, where I could turn and go down. Take that one picture with my camera tied to the ice ax of me standing in the ice winds of the afternoon with nothing above me, only the mountain ranges behind with their scattered snows. I knocked the balled-up snow from my crampons and started down. I had made a journey out of the day, saw the mountains below me, stood straight up in the high winds, and made a commitment at 12,000 feet to a place called The Heart.

CHAPTER FOUR

WE CELEBRATED CHRISTMAS 1956 AT OUR HOUSE AT OROTE, Guam. Celebrated the new year out at Umatac Bay where the green grass grows right up to the edges of sheltered reefs, where my father carried me on his back as we walked alongside the Filipino boys leading a water buffalo home. And I call that time of childhood, the Tumon Beach time. In the one photograph I have of us at Tumon Beach, Guam, I am wrapped in a large towel lying on the beach at my father's feet while he is standing wearing his sunglasses and smoking a cigar, dressed only in his swimming trunks. It was Christmas time. We were at the beach in the short days of winter, my father was playing General of the Beach as the orange glow of the tropical sunset caught the glow in our brown skin. I was his prisoner. I lit his cigar.

And in 1956 at Tumon Beach he floated me out on a raft, swimming like Tarzan, with the raft's rope in his teeth. He pulled me out to the reefs with my goggles on, my fingers pinching my nostrils, my head bent down into the waters, so that I could see the striped colored fish. At Nimitz Beach, Guam, he would swim

out to coral reefs with his tennis shoes on, pulling me behind him on the raft to find colored coral.

There was a Tumon Beach time in Chinatown before we started traveling throughout the Pacific. I remember that time because it was so late, because Chinatown was deserted, the two of us walked down the middle of the street at two in the morning looking for a place to eat. I was an outlaw in the dark night, walking alongside my father on the slippery brick streets of Chinatown. And in the bright fluorescent glow of that café, my father talked to me while we had a meal of noodles and won ton. There were a few old men sitting at the counter, but ours were the only voices in the café. He would drive me from Berkeley to Ocean Beach to let me shovel sand all day long in the gray days of San Francisco.

I stood on the front seat of our car as he drove on the bottom deck of the Bay Bridge with the trucks and trains. We were every noisy machine in the world then. The General driving a B-17 on the bottom deck of the Bay Bridge, breathing the cold, thin air of the last journey home. Crippled. Smoking. I call the pilot "Bobby," yell his name out, "Bobby! Do you think we'll make it?" We're flying at 100 feet above the water, flying a black B-17 named "Rita."

"Yeah," he says, "this is 'Rita' ain't it?" And my father is talking bad to me now and I know we'll make it. "Don't ever let me down, Rita!" he says. He looks over at me. "Yeah, outlaw, we'll make it. It's a clear day, and there ain't nothin' to run into out here over the ocean." We fly home on one engine, making a perfect crash landing. And we come home laughing, the General Bobby leaning down to whisper to me before we went into the house, "Now, it ain't polite to say ain't or yeah in front of Mother. You know what I mean, outlaw? Say, yeah."

I'm heading toward the Mariposa Grove time, where I saw wilderness for the first time, where my father drove through the tunnel redwood tree in the Mariposa Grove, Yosemite, with me, my mother, my uncle and my aunt, in the car. When he guided that old black Ford through the hole in the giant redwood, he set up the spirit in me for my own journeys, made sounds in my head for the poor towns of Idaho, out of the Rockies and into the desert between mountain ranges. One spring I skied across the Sierras in nine days, to come upon dreams of my great-grandfather when the coyote's cry pulled down the frozen air of the twilight. I could not see the sunset, but saw its colors reflected off the clouds into a band of orange against the snow-covered peaks. This was my coldest night as I again heard the coyote's howl touch a note in the failing light. And as I hiked out of the mountains with my skis resting over my shoulders I came upon the pure days of Bridgeport Valley, and the barren waters of Mono Lake. And driving home over the steep Sonora Pass road at night is a climb into a night darker than any night I've seen. I do not even see the black outline of mountain ranges.

And there was another time I thought of at 10,000 feet in the night of Sonora Pass. I was hiking on the 180-mile trail from Lake Tahoe to Yosemite Valley with a girl so much younger than myself we offended people. She was a dream girl, a patronizing blond-haired girl of fifteen. And in the dream about me I'm hiking with her alone, making up for those restless years, the lonely years of my grandfathers. A scout troop camped across the river and the scoutmaster sees us, sees how close she sleeps to me. I'm fiercely loyal to her. We're on the run through America.

When I was in college, kids would ask where I was from and I would answer Jackson Hole, Wyoming, when they were thinking Hong Kong. Raised by a song about buffalo and antelope, by a song about a home on the range. I was brought up in the shade of that giant redwood tunnel tree at Mariposa Grove, Big Trees, Yosemite National Park, by my father who was a man of journeys.

What matters about a time in Hilo, Hawaii, is what happened before that time. The day before my mother and I flew out of Guam, out of the humid morning, to begin the journey home to follow Father's hospital plane home, I remember my childhood from that time on rooted in a moment with Father in the hospital when all journeys end without speech. We arrived in Hilo in the middle of the night on a stopover rest sometime in early spring 1957. I woke up when the vibration of the props died, and I felt the bump of the wheels touch down. And when I'm driving at night now, I think of the time when that giant Pan American Globemaster touched down on Hilo, and of my mother pacing in the hotel room all night long while I slept. I was tired of traveling at the age of seven, and Hilo was the last stop before home. And that night was the longest night she would experience as my mother. Father was already in the hospital and we were following him home. Because of the resignation to waiting in that hotel room, the last day of the last journey home was worse than her own sickness eight years later. To only hope and wait was a sign of weakness for her, hoping was a sign of impatience. And when my father died, hope was gone, but patience was her only energy then. And in the eight years before her own death I saw no resignation to hope, no more midnight landings in Hilo.

I take my dream bride of fifteen now into the whole flux of my life; she patronizes her way into my future, I have explained my past, sought it out, told about the Tumon Beach time, the Mariposa Grove time, the Hilo time, Wyoming, the Orote house before spring 1957. And now in America I say to her that I have no place in America, after four generations there is nothing except what America tells me about the pride of being foreign, a visitor from a China I've never seen, never been to, never dream about, and never care about. Or, at best, here in my country I am still living at the fringe, the edge of China. So now I take this fifteen-year-old blond-haired body with me on the road. She is the shadow, the white ghost of all my love life; she is the true dream of my capture of America. She buys me breakfast at six in the morning in Elko, Nevada. And as we walk through the casino in Elko looking for breakfast, the gamblers ignore her and stare at me like I'm crazy. This is Chinese-America in Elko. I have steak and eggs for breakfast, she has a milkshake and fries.

My patronizing blond-haired, whining, pouting bride of fifteen, known to me as "The Body," is my whole responsibility to America. She is America. She tells me things about me that I am not. America patronizes me and loves me and tells me that I am the product of the richest and oldest culture in the history of the world. She credits me with all the inventions of modern life, when in fact I have nothing of my own in America. But I stay with her to get what I can out of her.

I do not like to linger on the summits of mountains. I do not take pride in standing on the summits of mountains, there is no dignity achieved by it. Had I climbed only one mountain in my life, I might have taken some pride in that as an accomplishment. It is an exercise of faith, of the heart, and once you've achieved that goal you have nothing to work for; it is a kind of disappointment to meet that goal. I do not consider death simply as tragedy, but rather the affirmation of life. When my father and mother died I considered myself at the summit of a mountain and out of all the advice I received in my youth I gave my spirit over to a woman who must have been a mountaineer in her own youth, and who said, "There is no time left for pride, for dignity, only to turn, without grieving, and to go."

And now when I dwell on my own grief for an instant, I like to think I'm on the road heading out to Wisconsin, where I loved a woman, where she now lives. Her own grandfather lit out from China, sailed over the Pacific, and fled from the West Coast to Wisconsin and set roots there. She gave me part of her life back there early one summer when I was still dreaming about grand-fathers, trying to pull all of my past together. She sends me pressed roses and lilies of the valley. And when I'm on the road at night, I am all of the romantic that I am, she plays the elusive spirit of my loving, she is the fresh smell of rain falling on the Wiscon-sin marshlands in summer. She tells me that it is bitingly cold in Wisconsin in the wintertime, but I know her only in early summer. When I'm on the road at night, she is that Wisconsin time when I held her close to me, hugging her in the sudden downpour, she is that Wisconsin time when I held her by that marsh bordering the green hidden lake and the rain came down into the thick forest growth. The air around us was claustro-phobic. Small drops of water trickled down off her hair, off her face, wetted down her blouse against her skin. I saw her breath-ing the sweet air around us. It was the calm rain after the thun-der, the rain comes straight down. But she is only the myth of the perfect day until I do get back to her home, she is the sum-mit I must turn to in the end.

In the dream about me I do not go back to her. But it will be some time before I get up there. I've got this thing going with my bride to straighten out America. I've told her all my stories, all my dreams about my grandfathers, my father and mother. My whole life story became her life story. She swears like I do, she names names like I do. She was the pilot that took over the controls when the real pilot keeled over and died in the movies. I gave her instructions from the ground. Talked her into a perfect landing.

She said she loved me. I didn't want her love. She said I saw her only from my point of view. She was right. In desperation she said, "You people are not polite, you should be more like . . ." She never finished the statement. She couldn't figure out whom we should be more like. Finally, she said, "Just go back home." I gave her the car. I was already at home.

I knew America by living away from it. I caught glimpses of it from Guam, that tropical, white, sandy piece of America. I lived it every day, every minute of the day. I saw what other boys in America saw, and I saw things they only imagined. The bombers, the fighters, the aircraft carriers, the submarines, and every time a ship or the air base had an open house my father took me.

My parents and I were invited as guests of the commander aboard a Chinese destroyer from Taiwan. When we got to where the ship was docked, I looked in horror at the slim gray destroyer and said, "That's not a Chinese destroyer. It looks just like one of ours."

We had lunch with the commander and officers and after lunch the sailors took me around the ship, gesturing in sign language when I knew what all the stuff was. They showed me the engine room, the depth charge rack, the bridge. They showed me the inside of a big gun turret and kept saying, "Boom! Boom!" and I kept saying, "I know. I know." I had a great time and they didn't even have to speak or understand English. We saw a movie with the crew called *The Long, Long Trailer*. It was in English, but it must have been the funniest movie they ever saw because they laughed all the way through it.

These guys were Chinese and I knew then I wasn't one of them. It didn't bother me when I was a kid and the other kids called me Chinese, but occasionally I was called a Chinaman. The way they said it I knew they knew something I didn't know. The Chinaman was something right out of science fiction for me. When you called someone a Chinaman it didn't mean Chinese. It was a mutant name dragged up out of America's need to name names. When the Chinese came here they were no longer just Chinese because they threatened the white labor force, a way of life. They wanted something out of America, a way of life of their own. A "Chinaman" threatened history, culture, and language the way a "Jap" loosed chaos on the world. Being Chinese meant you kept to your history, your culture, your language from a country you've never been to. In the dream about me, I know my name.

In the dream about me they give me my bride back. I tell her about the real America where I saw it when I was six and seven. I tell her about a kid on Guam, how he used to go to the outdoor movies with his parents and sit with all the sailors on benches out in the warm night, how he didn't see a TV until 1957, when he came home. He grew up on Jerry Lewis movies, and Francis the Talking Mule movies. Out there in the warm night, I tell her about how I looked for fireflies in the night.

In the dream about me I get the girl I wanted when I was fifteen. She is the patronizing, slim, long-legged, blond-haired, full-breasted, wholesome, innocent, fifteen-year-old, high school, whining, teaser of a cheerleader. She is pouting, telling me about how mad she is at her parents, how they try and make her live the life they lived. I tell her she can live the life I've lived. I tell her about a kid on Guam whose father brings home a tattered Charlie McCarthy puppet. He tells his father, "I don't play with dolls."

"But this is not a doll. His name is Charlie McCarthy and he talks." His father puts his hand through the back of the puppet, spins the head around, and pulls the string that moves the mouth.

"Hi, my name is Charlie McCarthy. I'm glad to meet you." The mouth claps open and shut. The arm pushes out to shake hands. The head spins all the way around. The kid shakes his hand. His mother comes over and sits in front of Charlie McCarthy, and Charlie says, "Hi, baby. What's for dinner? I'm hungry."

She says in Chinese, "Broccoli with beef, steamed fish, soup, and rice." She winks at Charlie.

Charlie says, "*Ngoh m'sick gong tong hua.* Or in other words, sweetheart, I don't speak no Chinese. I don't care no how what's on the table, just take me to it. Time to chow down, kid. Let's go wash our hands."

I named my Charlie McCarthy doll "Freddy." Other kids were going around telling me I couldn't name him Freddy because his name was already Charlie McCarthy. So I told them I called him Freddy for short. It was his Chinese name. I got pretty good at talking with my teeth clamped down into a pasted grin on my face. My mother made him a new suit out of pieces of leftover Chinese silk from one of her dresses. Man, he looked sharp in a red silk suit, white shirt, and a tie my father had won with a map of Guam on it. And Freddy was how I learned a few words of Chinese. Nobody had a Charlie McCarthy doll on the island that could speak Chinese. My mother taught me Chinese by telling the words to Freddy, and Freddy would say them to me, and I would say them back to my mother in English and Chinese.

We had lessons in the kitchen while my mother was fixing dinner. Between walking from the refrigerator to the stove she'd cast a glance at Freddy and teach the numbers to him from one to ten.

"*Yi*," said Mother.

"*Yi*," said Freddy.

"One. *Yi!*" I said.

"*Er*."

"Ergh." It came up through the teeth from the throat, like a cough.

"Two. *Er*," I said. Freddy nodded.

"*San*."

"*San*," Freddy said when the tip of my tongue hit the roof of my mouth.

"Three. *San*."

"*Sz*."

"*Sz*." *Sz* was like spitting water between your two front teeth.

"Four. *Sz*," I said swallowing and licking my dry lips from so much air pressing through the teeth.

"*Wu*."

"*Wu*," Freddy said, curling up the sides of my tongue.

"Five. *Wu*."

"*Lyou*."

"*Lyou*," Freddy said, making my tongue flap through the one syllable like a wave in the bottle of my mouth.

"Six. *Lyou*," I said as Freddy started to snore.

"Wake up, Freddy. It's time for *chi*."

"Eeegads. Chee! Take it away, kid," he said, his mouth clapping like the hooves of horses.

71

"Seven. *Chi*," I said, relaxing the muscles of my jaw.

"*Ba*." My mother smiled at this one, because Freddy couldn't say *ba* without closing the lips of my mouth.

Freddy looked at me with his mouth open, "Are you ready for this one kid? Here goes, *ba*." I couldn't do it without bringing my lips together. If I said *ba* while smiling it sounded like what a soldier says when he's been shot.

"Eight. *Ba*," I said.

"That was real nice," Freddy said.

"Thanks, buddy."

"Only two more to go, boys," she said and continued with "*Jyou*."

"*Jyou*."

"Nine. *Jyou*," I said as I flexed the muscles of my jaw.

"*Shr*."

"*Shr*." The air whistles through my bottom row of teeth.

"Ten. *Shr*."

"Okay, Freddy, say them all at once," she said while stopping all her work, because this was what she enjoyed about the lesson above all else. When Freddy said all the numbers it sounded like the soundtrack to the landing on the beaches of Iwo Jima.

After that, learning Chinese was really a challenge. My mother told me I had to learn a few words of Chinese because we were going to visit my grandmother in Hong Kong for a few weeks. So me and Freddy learned all the necessary words to get by, including *ngoh m'sick gong tong hua*. When we got there it took me a long time before I could say any Chinese words without my teeth freezing into that plastered grin. It was the way I learned Chinese from that Chinaman, Charlie McCarthy. I knew I had hit something right because in all those war movies showing the bad Japs tearing up the Pacific Islands, screaming down out of the skies as kamikazis, yelling *Banzai* in the jungles of each Pacific tropical island, they, in all those movies whispered, ordered, yelled, shouted, screamed, made speeches in English and Japanese with their teeth clamped into that grin I knew so well.

She sits in a chair in front of me, one foot is up on the seat of the chair while the other stays on the floor, her chin is resting on the knee of the raised leg. She is wearing her white blouse from gym class, a plaid Catholic school pleated skirt, white socks, and saddle shoes. She has been listening to my story. She is named after an American doll. She's got a name like Becky or Nancy Ann. She laughs at my story and says, "Who's Charlie McCarthy?" I've become more impatient. She is beginning to waste my time. I say let's go and park somewhere.

"How come you never look at me when I talk to you?"

"Take us somewhere dark and lonely."

It was a dark night in America when my mother and I flew home, touched down in San Francisco, came home from Guam.

We fly home on one engine, making a perfect crash landing. "Don't ever let me down, Rita!" he says. He looks over at me, "Yeah, outlaw, we'll make it. It's a clear day, and there ain't nothing to run into out here over the ocean."

It was dawn when we turned up the fur collars on our jackets and slipped down into the frosted seats of the cockpit, strapped on the radio and ear phones, buckled up and ran the check. Bobby was the best there was. Squadron leader. We had a tail gunner that always got sick from facing backwards. We had a bombardier who used to build shooting galleries. I was still reading the checklist with the flashlight stuck under my arm, and blowing warm air in my hands, when Bobby pushed the starter for engine one. Heard it cough once and start. He smiled at me and said, "Good ol' faithful. That's Rita's best one. That's the one that'll get us through the clutch someday."

In another instant I had my gloves on. Then his thumbs-up signal to me. A glance amid the drone of the engines. The plane was shaking, straining to move forward, the wings flexing. I slid back my window and looked out at engines three and four. Said to him, "Let's get Rita up there! Go!" We led off a line of B-17s named The Lady's Aces, Buttercup, Sylvia, Las Vegas, Baby Doll, The Danger, and The King of Hearts.

"Okay. Take over, outlaw. Time for coffee. Keep them tight." We circled back around the island and headed out to sea.

Yes, out there on Guam was where I stuck my head down into that cockpit of that crashed fighter behind our house at Orote. Looked down into the stale air of ghosts, afraid of seeing bad blood, afraid of seeing a piece of bone on a lever still guiding the plane up for more altitude. The dials and needles pointed to zero. They pointed their way home. The piece of wing I was standing on moaned when I lifted myself off it and eased myself down into the seat, brushing away the dust and broken glass. I kneeled down on the seat, grasped the bent and charred lever in front of me, heard my heart beating as I flicked one of the toggle switches. Breathed out, held it out, and with no oxygen in my lungs, moved another switch on. Took another breath. I heard the scream of my imagination catching the branches of the trees in front of me, heard the wings tearing off into the blaze of trees, felt myself slammed into the explosion of trees breaking open. I said to someone, "Can I get out now? Can I get out now?" There's a faded yellow sign on the wing that says, "Step Here."

Rita was going down, sending out a stream of black smoke behind her. Bobby said, "Jump." Everybody went out and we were losing altitude and he told me to jump and he'd be right behind me, but of course he wasn't. When we touched down in San Francisco that was the beginning of life with Mother. I had to seek out friends to keep the imagination running at full pace. After a cousin and I saw "Pork Chop Hill" we played "Pork Chop Hill" all day long for a week. I wore a pair of Colt .45s, a Winchester slung over my back, a bow slung over the other shoulder, three plastic hand grenades stuck in the bottom holes of my shirt, two Jolly Roger Buccaneer rubber knives stuck in my belt, and a sailor's hat on my head. My cousin carried a submachine gun, a .38 that shot suction cup darts, a Pancho Villa bullet belt slung over his shoulder, the suction cupped arrows to my bow, and a fire chief's helmet on his head.

There was a time in the Sierras when I was skiing over them in spring. I camped at the edge of a wide meadow and heard a plane in the night laboring over the mountains, heard it come down low, droning out an echo through this meadow surrounded by mountains, heard it in my dreams first as the touch of a melodious note in this cathedral of snows. I sat up in the cold freezing night and saw the wing lights of that plane come down low over the meadow, then lean out into a gradual turn to the west toward some city. The moon was covering the snows of the deep meadow. The plane's distant throbbing was absorbed into the powdery surface of the mountains.

There were sheets of ice clinging to the wings. One engine was sputtering. My teeth were chattering. All the crew had come forward and were huddled in the cockpit behind us for warmth, stamping their feet, clapping their gloved hands together. Icicles hung from my fur collar. We needed another 300 feet to clear the range and with three engines that would be difficult. The engines coughed, sputtered.

"Don't let it die, outlaw, keep it going!"

"It's dead. Frozen," I said.

"Okay, boys, time for exercise! Unload everything heavy! We gotta get up, otherwise we're going through!"

The mountains got bigger and bigger. Bobby said look for a dip in the range so we can sneak by one of the peaks, fly down-range and slip through another gap, and bring the bomber down to warm air, let the engines unfreeze. When the plane got so close you could make out large boulders and gapping crevasses in the glaciers, and when it was still not enough altitude, we were told we didn't have a "Chinaman's Chance" in hell of getting through. Bobby found a way to get through and down into the fertile farmlands of Europe. We were cheering all the way, hugging each other, then looked for landmarks for the way home. They made Rita into a weather plane after the war, painted the tail orange, and gave her to the navy.

It was that dark night in 1952 when my father and I were walking down the brick sweets of Chinatown looking for a place to eat. At two in the morning there were a few old men walking along the streets in heavy dark overcoats, and most of the stores were lighted. These streets and alleys smell of discarded food in the gutters, smell of fish scales washed out across the sidewalk into the gutters, and in the dark night this town smells wet, damp, penetrating. You walk carefully through this town at night, looking for a place to eat. There is a pulse at night, when the neon lights shine in the scales of the street. You never drive through this town, only walk.

"Can we go there sometime?" my bride had said. "Will you take me there for lunch sometime? Coffee? Anything."

"They make terrible coffee there." I was standing above her, looking down.

"I don't care what we have. I just want to see it."

"What do you want to see?"

"Just see Chinatown."

"Okay. We'll drive through sometime."

She stood up and straightened her dress. "My brother used to be a gas station mechanic."

"So did I."

"You ought to meet him sometime. He's a nice guy. He's done a lot of things. I used to try and be like him."

"So did I."

She laughed. "You don't even know him." She brushed her hair back. "I used to follow him on his paper route."

"A girl in my class named Katie who was the daughter of a famous writer used to follow me on mine when I was nine."

"My brother used to be a Boy Scout."

"I was too. And a Cub Scout."

"He played Little League baseball."

"So did I."

"He was on the high school football team."

"I was on the water polo and swimming team."

"He has a letterman's jacket."

"So do I."

"He lettered three times."

"I lettered five times and was voted most valuable player."

". . . at a Chinese high school?"

"Your brother went to a Chinese high school?"

"No, stupid. Did you go to a Chinese high school?"

"What's a *Chi-neese* high school?"

"You know what I mean. A high school in Chinatown."

"I was the only Chinaman at an all-white high school and I never tell anyone about those years."

"How come you were so athletic? You don't look athletic."

"I was a poor sport."

"Can we go there today?"

"Where? A Chinese high school?"

"Chinatown. I'll wear that dress you like so much."

"Wear pants."

In the dream about me when I was staring into the darkness of my aunt's children's shop, I saw the reflection of the old trolley cars that rolled up and down the main street of Berkeley, I saw our old house down there on Bancroft Way where my father popped popcorn for me without the top on the pan. And I saw my bride sitting in the car waiting for me to start traveling, start moving out on the road.

When my mother died she left me in pursuit of myself at fifteen, left me without humility. There is everything at fifteen. When she died I knew my own violence, my anger, my desires, my own force to compete. I grew up away from Chinatown, away from relatives, away from America, yet in it all the time. I had only the two of them to keep pace with me. In the dream about me at Tumon Beach, at six years old I commit outrageous acts of heroism, at ten in Little League I am the boy wonder in the major leagues, at eleven in the Boy Scouts I save the lives of girls from the grip of death, at fifteen I am violent, arrogant because I know what I want out of my life. I want to pursue life, I want life to be difficult for me. I want to test myself. I want to feel like I'm being chased on the road at night. There is the glare of headlights at the back of my head, the rearview mirror casts a strip of light across my eyes.

You are more alone at fifteen than any other age. No lovers. Without a father, mother, brother, sister, there is nothing except your own energy that keeps loneliness and pity at arm's length.

And every day after school I swam dozens of laps, played water polo to exhaustion. I kept my appetite at a peak, I slept soundly all night long, I never let up a single day. After a water polo game, I pulled myself out of the pool by my limp arms, my back, neck, and face red from sweating in the water. When I am awarded the Most Valuable Player trophy a year after my mother's death, my coach says to a crowd of athletes, parents, and teachers that I am the first Chinese in the history of this high school to receive this award in any sport, and they applaud. My heart is beating fast, I am short of breath, I begin my steps up to the platform where he is speaking. "Rainsford Chan has more drive and more determination than any member of the team . . ." he says in a hollow voice that I do not recognize. I am still walking through the auditorium, I am sweating, my shirt sticks to my back like the hot humid days on Guam, my feet are soaking with sweat in my hot shoes. ". . . this is an award for more than doing your best, to pull a team together . . ." I say, I whisper, I do not want this award, I don't need it, I need to keep running. ". . . Rainsford is a credit to the team, to this school, to his race . . ." I am there, finally, everybody is applauding, and I am dizzy from the heat, on the stage, in the spotlights I need air, I take the award, I shake my coach's hand, I nod into the stage's spotlights at the darkened audience. ". . . I can say that I am proud of you, and I know the school and your family is proud of you . . ." I will never admit it.

CHAPTER FIVE

I

MY GRANDFATHER'S ISLAND IS ANGEL ISLAND. IT WAS THERE
that he almost died and that makes it his island.

There are two islands in San Francisco Bay which contain
ruined buildings with doors four inches thick. The islands are
Alcatraz and Angel Island. Alcatraz is a National Park and Angel
Island is a California State Park. Both were places of great sad-
ness and great pain.

During Christmas 1969, an Indian man in whom I saw my
grandfather showed me my grandfather's face.

I am inclined to believe in ghosts because islands in California are places of waiting and the waiting is what destroys
people.

I saw the man that Christmas while I was leaning on a four-
inch-thick door that led to an isolation cell. I was facing out into
the main corridor of the cell block on Alcatraz. Behind me, inside
the isolation cell, were two women sleeping in sleeping bags laid
on top of newspapers on the concrete floor. I was shivering and

felt cold and damp all over. The cold moved in on me through the concrete and the salt air etched its way through my skin, attacking my bones until they ached. Each night for the last three nights I woke up and wandered into the corridor to sit near a kerosene lantern with a few others believing light had something to do with warmth. And each night I noticed the old man sitting against a wall between cell doors. He was smoking as usual. We never spoke. As I seated myself on a piece of newspaper, he stood up and walked over to me and stood over me holding his enormous wool jacket in his hand.

"You know, people say I look Chinese," he said.

I nodded a little trying to shake off the shivers. He held out his jacket.

"Oh, ah, no. I've got a jacket on. You probably need it."

"Take it off and sit on it and put this one on."

I did what he said and he sat down next to me. I moved over to make room on the newspaper. Both of us leaned against the wall and faced out into the corridor as we spoke. The jacket was about ten sizes too big and smelled of cigarettes.

"People say I look Chinese," he repeated.

I looked at him in the dim light. He did look Chinese. "Where are you from?" I asked.

"Acoma."

"Lots of Chinese in New Mexico?"

He started laughing and lit up another cigarette. "Where are you from?"

"Berkeley."

"Where are you from originally?"

"Berkeley."

"How long you been here?"

"Three days."

"No. How long you been in the United States?"

"All my life."

"You mean you ain't born in China?"

"What do you mean? Don't I look like I come from Gallup?"

"You ain't Navajo. You Chinese. You like me."

"You ain't Chinese, though."

"My ancestors came from China thirty thousand years ago and settled in Acoma Pueblo."

"Is that why you look Chinese?"

"Naw, my grandfather was Chinese."

"Your grandfather was Chinese?" I turned to look at the old man and tore our newspaper.

"He wandered into New Mexico and married a widow before anyone knew he was Chinese." He crushed his cigarette into the floor and smiled to himself. I was looking at his face more closely. He started chuckling then turned to me. "You pretty lucky"—he pointed into the room I was sleeping in—"to sleep in isolation with two women."

"Oh, they're just friends from school."

"That one, Sandy, the Nez Percé, looks Japanese."

"Yeah, me and your grandfather . . ."

"What does she call you?"

"What do you mean?"

"What's your name?"

"Rainsford."

"Rainsford?"

"That's my name. Rainsford."

"Sounds like the name of a town."

"It was. My great-grandfather lived there."

"It was in California?"

"Did you ever hear of it?"

He appeared to think carefully for a while. Then he said, "We used to call it Ah-Caht-Cho."

"Ah-Caht-Cho? What does that mean?"

"What are you doing here?" he said.

"Huh?"

"What are you doing here? This isn't your battle or your land."

"I'm part of this land too."

"You should be out looking for your place, your home. This is part of mine." He paused for a moment to take another cigarette out. He couldn't find a match and put the cigarette back into the pack. "If you came here because of the two women, then you're as smart as my grandfather. But you got your own land to find."

"But I live here."

"That's what I mean. This is your country. Go out and make yourself at home." The man chuckled to himself. Then took a breath like he was going to let me in on the joke, but he only chuckled again. "You know what my grandfather did for a living?"

"The Chinese one?"

"Yes."

"Railroad worker? Miner?"

"No. He was a bone collector."

"A what?"

"A bone collector."

"He collected bones?"

As the old man nodded he looked in the direction of a young man carrying a rifle and walking toward us. As he came nearer

83

the old man asked him for a light. He stopped and drew out a small box of matches and tossed them to the old man saying, "Here's a whole box. Keep warm. Merry Christmas."

"You said your Chinese grandfather collected bones. What kind of bones?"

"Chinese bones, of course."

". . . of Chinese?"

"Yes."

"Yes?"

The old man nodded his head again. Then he said, "Haven't you ever heard of the bone collectors?"

I shook my head.

"You know what a tong is?"

"Yeah."

"You sure you're Chinese?"

"I'm as Chinese as your grandfather."

"Well, in my grandfather's days the tongs hired men like him to travel around looking for the bones of dead Chinamen so that the tong could send them back to China."

"What was your grandfather doing in New Mexico?"

"There was some Chinamen there . . . a graveyard somewhere and my grandfather went around asking people who might have known them, you know, known their names. Probably some Indian bones got sent back to China by mistake." He laughed and brought a hand down on my shoulder.

"Well, you Indians came from China thirty thousand years ago."

"Yes, you might be right." He took a drag off his cigarette and then crushed it out on the floor in front of us. He looked up and pointed at the walls, "Look at this. These things we've painted on the walls, claiming this piece of land." He paused for a moment. I was feeling warm now, even tired and drowsy. "It's funny how people write on walls. Most times it's a desperate and lonely job. Look inside some of these cells."

I was letting him talk, his deep voice almost making the air warm and dry.

"There's an island," he said, "next to this one, you know, where they used to keep prisoners of war and Chinese. Some of the buildings are still standing. I wonder what's written on those walls."

"Chinese were kept on Angel Island?"

"You didn't know that? I'm more Chinese than you are. I said before you got to find your own land, you know, where your people have been. Like Angel Island, like Rainsford, California."

"Where is Rainsford, California? Do you know where in the Sierra?"

"You better get some sleep now. We'll talk tomorrow."

I went to bed and forgot to take off his jacket. When I went back to the door, he was gone. I laid it out like a blanket over me. I slept soundly. I dreamed my father and I were walking through a forest of redwood trees. I talked like my father, I laughed like him, I smelled like him. And I knew then that I was only my father's son, that he was Grandfather's son and Grandfather was Great-Grandfather's son and that night we were all the same man.

I dreamed all this underneath the wool jacket, not knowing the old man had made up the name "Ah-Caht-Cho" after someone's nighttime sneeze that echoed in the cell block while we were talking.

It was barely light out when he came to get his jacket. He woke me with a gentle nudge. "Rainsford," he said, while lifting the weight of his jacket off me. When I opened my eyes, he bent over to look me in the face. "Rainsford, an island is the saddest kind of land there is."

II

"Drifting alone in the ocean it suddenly passed autumn."
—Angel Island

NOW AFTER SEEKING OUT ALL THE WRONG NAMES TO CALL myself, I've been to those places that can destroy me, I've felt those places overcome me without violence, only my own dreaming brought it on until I was able to say that I am violent and I sought out those places, making them mine.

Now I know that my grandfather's land was an island. He was born in San Francisco but his father, my great-grandfather, sent him back to China for safety. It was 1917 when he came back. And in 1917 Grandfather's island was called Angel Island.

My grandfather's land sits in the middle of San Francisco Bay directly in the path of the fog that flows in from the Golden Gate. The fog meets Angel Island and moves around it to hold it and silence it. When the fog lifts and retreats to the sea it will often leave a halo around the peaks of Angel Island.

On the north side of the island, at Winslow Cove, there is a building called P-317—the U.S. Justice Department Immigration detention center for Chinese immigrants. A chain-link fence surrounds the building. All the windows are broken yet the frames for the small panes of glass are still in position. Some windows are half open.

There is a movement about the place that gives off sound like sleeping gives off dreams, like a haunted house moves people to realize that life still exists within. The sounds I heard as a child in dreams made me deaf but never woke me. Hearing voices wakes me.

I have to bend back the fence to get near the building. I walk through and release the fence and it springs back into place and rattles against the pole that holds it. There is broken glass everywhere, even on the stairs leading to the door. After I make my way past the sounds under my-feet of old wood rotten from the ocean air mixed with breaking glass, I am standing at an open door looking in.

III

ONCE INSIDE, YOU WILL SEE THAT THE ROOM IS LIT WITH BARE bulbs hung from the ceiling. You will see that the room is filled with men, women, and children. There are two lines—men and young boys in one and women and a few very young children in the other. An officer stands between the two lines. Behind a large counter there is an officer for each line. There is some shuffling but no talking except for the two officers behind the counter. You will see that we are dressed in drab jackets, some men are wearing long coats with black pants underneath, others are wearing regular work clothes, and many are wearing flat-brim black hats.

You will know why you're standing in line with me. I am my grandfather come back to America after having been raised in China. My father is dead so I've had to assume someone else's name and family in order to legally enter the country. All this information about my new family has been memorized. All my sons after me will have my assumed name.

I was not allowed to ever leave the building, even to go outside. Husbands were not allowed to see their wives or children who were kept in another part of the building. We ate in different shifts. There were riots in the mess hall and the main building. We had given up everything to come to this country. Many were former citizens. If you ran your fingers across the walls at night in the dark, your fingers would be filled with the splinters of poems carved into the walls. Maybe there is a dim light to help see what your fingers feel. But you can only read, "Staying on this island, my sorrow increases with the days/my face is growing sallow and body is getting thin," before your fingers give out following the grooves and gouges of the characters.

Sometimes the morning will show you someone has hanged himself in the night, someone who could no longer bear the waiting, or the interrogation, or failing the interrogation—someone waiting to be sent back to China. Everyone knows how to hang yourself. There are no nails or hooks high enough to hang a piece of cloth from and leap from a stool to a quick death. There is only one way—to tie your piece of cloth on one of those big nails about four and a half feet off the floor, lean against the wall to brace yourself, and bend your knees and hold them up off the floor. Then your bones will be collected and placed on the open seas.

IV

I HAVE MEMORIZED SOMEONE ELSE'S FAMILY HISTORY, TAKEN someone else's name and suppressed everything that I have chronicled for myself. The questions begin in the Interrogation Room. It is a room blocked off from the light. The windows are painted black. One immigration officer has a list of questions in his hand and the other has a file folder in front of him with the data given by relatives years ago.

QUESTION	How large is your village?
ANSWER	It has fifty houses.
QUESTION	How many rows of houses are there?
ANSWER	Ten rows.
QUESTION	Which way does the village face and where is the head?
ANSWER	It faces east and the head is south.
QUESTION	Where is your house located?
ANSWER	Second house, third row, counting from the south.
QUESTION	Do you know who lived in that house before your family?
ANSWER	I do not remember.
QUESTION	How many houses in your row?
ANSWER	Five.
QUESTION	Do all of the houses in your row touch each other?
ANSWER	None of them do.
QUESTION	How far apart are they?
ANSWER	About six feet.
QUESTION	What were the sleeping arrangements in your house when you were last in China?
ANSWER	My mother, all my brothers, and I occupied the south bedroom.
QUESTION	How many beds are in the south bedroom?
ANSWER	Sometimes two, and sometimes three.
QUESTION	Please explain that statement.
ANSWER	When the weather gets warm, we use three.
QUESTION	How many steps lead to your front door?
ANSWER	None.
QUESTION	Is there a clock in your house?

ANSWER   Yes.

QUESTION Describe it.

ANSWER   It is wood on the outside. It is brass with a white porcelain face. It has brass numbers.

QUESTION Where did your mother buy provisions?

ANSWER   She buys at the Tin Wo Market.

QUESTION How far and in what direction is that from your village?

ANSWER   One or two lis west.

QUESTION How many of your brothers have attended school?

ANSWER   All my brothers.

QUESTION Did they attend the same school with you?

ANSWER   Yes.

QUESTION When did your youngest brother start school?

ANSWER   The beginning of this year.

QUESTION When did your oldest brother start school?

ANSWER   When he was eleven years old.

QUESTION When did you quit school?

ANSWER   I attended school for six months this year, then I quit.

QUESTION Who told you to quit?

ANSWER   My mother. She told me to prepare myself to go to the United States.

QUESTION When did you first learn that you were to come to the United States of America?

ANSWER   About the time my mother told me to quit school.

The officer asking the questions stops for a moment. He puts down the paper he's been reading from and draws out a tobacco pouch and begins to roll a cigarette for himself. He rises from his chair and goes to the window. He licks his cigarette and draws a match out from his pocket and lights his cigarette. The second officer has stopped writing whatever he was writing and puts down his pencil. The first one begins scraping the black paint from a small section of the window. He pulls out his pocket knife, unfolds it, and continues scraping until he has a small peep hole. "It's a nice day outside," he says to no one. The room fills with the cigarette smoke. He continues to look out the hole in the window and absent-mindedly is folding and unfolding his pocket knife. "Where does your mother receive her mail?" He asks with his back still turned to me.

"I don't know."

"Who goes after the mail?"

"My mother."

"Where do you suppose she goes to get it?"

"I don't know."

"Describe your mother."

"She is medium in height and slim in build. She has black hair. She is exuberant, graceful, and stubborn." I see her on no particular day in my mind. Her hair is set in a fashionable wave. She always wore red lipstick, not brilliant red but a darker shade. She used eyebrow pencil even though she didn't need it. She was always looking at her clothes to see if everything was in place, picking lint off, brushing her hand over the material as if to smooth out a wrinkle. She was doing that now as she crossed the street. She had extravagant taste in clothes, not flashy, but suits made of Italian knits, cashmere sweaters, elegant slips.

"Does your mother wear any jewelry?"

"Yes."

"Describe it."

"It is a dark green jade bracelet. She wears it on her right wrist. I can hear her working around the house when she has it on because it knocks against everything she touches. I've felt it touching my skin many times."

The officer turns from the window to face me. He steps toward me, but I do not see him move toward me. I'm gazing out of the small hole he's carved in the window.

"Have you ever seen a photograph of your father?"

"Yes. Yes, it was taken on a day like today. He is seated in a wooden chair on a lawn somewhere next to a wooden table with a heart-shaped hole . . ." I see my father sleeping on a cot. It is night and the air around me is brilliantly cold. There is snow outside.

Then the poor men filled the island with their smells, filled the yellow glow of the bare light in the building. Their fists rose like clubs. When I smelled the rotting wood of the building, I rose with them. I moved with them through the barracks, screaming at the doors until the taste of metal came to my tongue. We beat at the steel doors until they broke loose from the wooden building. Then water came rushing in, pushing us back. Ocean water from a fire hose pushed at us until we were all huddled in the corners of the bunk room. The doors closed again.

After the riot of blood, a man was beaten and thrown into isolation. And beaten again and again until I could hear his flesh break like glass, cutting him deeper and the salt of his sweat moved like dark worms in his wound.

On days like today, the glass is merely under my feet and I pick the pieces up like I'm collecting bones. This is my home base, my Rainsford, California. I place the glass in a small pile on the floor and rise up to the window. On days like today, I will remember the time I took the rotting wooden windowsill in my hands and tore it to shreds. It crumbled like bone marrow. The window is open.

On days like today, I hear someone moving through the chainlink fence, something she's wearing strikes a note on the fence post and as the vibration fades away, she moves through.

CHAPTER SIX

THIS CHRONICLING OF MY LIFE SHOULD BE GIVEN THE NAME OF a place. A place for friends, family, and lovers. A place I can see all the way home. A clearing full of sun. A stronghold that doesn't keep me in but pushes me away from it and makes me survive. And today, after 125 years of our life here, I do not want just a home that time allowed me to have. America must give me legends with spirit. I take myths to name this country's canyons, dry riverbeds, mountains, after my father, grandfather, and great-grandfather. We are old enough to haunt this land like an Indian who laid down to rest and his body became the outline of the horizon. See his head reclining, that peak is his nose, that cliff his chin, and his folded arms are summits.

I name a canyon after my father as if he were five hundred years old. There is a whole nation there and the legend says that the ocean was my father's lover. Her spirit rides into the canyon at night like the sound of wind, yet there is no movement, only the dignity of his loving.

In this canyon I heard my great-grandfather walking through

the deep white sand. His walking was like short breaths of wind that stopped at my ears. Then I was in Reno waiting to take the train home to San Francisco. It was 1875. "Enough time," said Great-Grandfather, "to see legends." I said the names of stations and towns like prayers, as if they belonged to me: Reno, Verdi, Essex, Bronco. We moved into California and passed Boca, Prosser Creek, Proctor's, then into Truckee. Out of Truckee along Donner Creek, we ascended the side of cliffs, above canyons to Donner Summit, 195 miles from San Francisco. There were no legends there, only the winters and the deaths. "My bitterness," Great-Grandfather said, "is not myth or legend."

Down into Summit Valley, and along the canyon walls I saw myself running down the rocky sides of that canyon as fast as the wind moved down through the tops of tall trees. I came running down into a meadow of new grass that had my mother's fragrance. There were prayers here that meant "home." Down toward the Sacramento Valley, the train does not stop unless signaled. We are buried in every town: Cascade, Tamarack, Cisco, Emigrant Gap, Blue Canyon, China Ranch, Shady Run, Dutch Flat, and Gold Run.

One day in early spring here, I skied down into the north fork of the American River. It was a cold day. I was coasting downhill into a canyon. My narrow wooden skis made a clattering noise whenever I crossed patches of ice in the dark shady spots. I picked up speed passing from shade to light between trees. My skis were clattering, flexing, and shuddering over large sections of glare ice until I broke into an open treeless slope. I was skiing through soft powder snow and there was just the faintest sound of my gliding, like Great-Grandfather's walking through sand.

"All of us," Great-Grandfather said, "will rise up to greet you."

I gathered speed down this slope and heard only the air pass by my ears until the cold day made them ache. When I stopped for a rest I shook the snow from my pants and boots. I stamped my skis into the soft powder and heard my father's voice. He called me by my nickname. And I started off again down my father's canyon to claim this river for myself. My father is in every canyon I've journeyed into in the West.

I could not see the river when I got to the edge of it. It had tunneled under the snow. Only its muffled sound told me where it ran. I poked a hole through the thin crust of snow with my ski pole and saw the dark swift water beneath me.

The train passed Clipper Gap, Auburn, Newcastle, Penrhyn, Piño, Rocklin, Junction, Antelope, Arcade, and Sacramento, ninety miles from San Francisco. It is a smooth ride all the way home now through Davisville, Tremont, Dixon, Batavia, Elmira, Fairfield, Army Point, Benecia, Port Costa, Valona, Vallejo Junction, Tormey, Pinole, Sobrante, San Pablo, and Oakland. And home where I remembered all these names and repeated them down in Aquatic Park in Berkeley. I remembered my father sitting in the back seat of our car, while I stood on the front seat counting and naming the boxcars that passed by the factories. I have memorized all these towns and stations. Each town is a day in a journal, an entry in a diary, a letter, or prayer. And down in my father's canyon near Gold Run, where I made a journey out of the day, where I have found a stronghold, where I sang, prayed, and wrote: "We are old enough to haunt this land like an Indian who laid down to rest and his body became the outline of the horizon. This is my father's canyon. See his head reclining! That peak is his nose, that cliff his chin, and his folded arms are summits."

DISCUSSION QUESTIONS

THE INDIVIDUALS WHO ORIGINALLY SUGGESTED THESE DISCUS-
sion questions are denoted in parenthetical references.

1

How did the building of the Central Pacific Railroad by the Chinese influence the identity or portrayal of Chinese Americans? (Professor Johnson Cheu, Michigan State University)

2

In chapter five, Rainsford Chan meets an American Indian man on Alcatraz who tells him to find his own island (Angel Island). What is the significance of this meeting in relation to the narration of *Homebase* as a Chinese American novel? At the end of the novel, Rainsford claims the landscape of California through the blood and sweat of Chinese American labor. Consider this in the context of American Indian sovereignty movements. Analyze Wong's use of images of American Indians in counteracting the image of Asian Americans as perpetual foreigners. (Professor Wei Ming Dariotis, San Francisco State University)

3

If you have read Leslie Marmon Silko's novel, *Ceremony*, what do you think is the reciprocal relationship (along the foreigner/settler—indigenous/sovereign axis) of Asian Americans and American Indians in each other's creative fictions about being American? (Professor Wei Ming Dariotis, San Francisco State University)

4

What does Shawn Wong mean when he uses the word "violence" in *Homebase*? Be clear about the definitions and natures of the violence that the work seems to offer. It may be useful to consider some of the following: who controls the violence; who receives it; whether the violence is represented as a 'positive' or 'negative'; whether it is connected with race, gender, or class; whether it is exercised or merely threatened; what is gained or lost through violence; whether the violence is physical, psychological, or both. (Professor Stephen Sumida, University of Washington)

5

Homebase implies or calls for "inclusion" as opposed to "exclusion" and alienation of the ethnic and racial subject: in the
novel, the Chinese American protagonist actively asserts that
the United States is his "home." Discuss how the novel nego-
tiates the difference between inclusion and exclusion of Chinese from American culture and society. (Professor Stephen
Sumida, University of Washington)

6

Professor Sau-ling Wong writes in *Reading Asian American
Literature: From Necessity to Extravagance* (1993), "Without
explicitly linking [Rainsford Chan's] social rejection with
the large-scale, legislated persecution of early Chinese immigrants . . . Shawn Wong nevertheless shows a continuity between
past and present by lyrically interweaving the two." Discuss the
use of time in *Homebase* and how the history of the Chinese
America and the personal history of Rainsford Chan were combined in one narration.

7

In an essay by Professor Bill Brown, "How to Do Things with
Things (A Toy Story)," published in *Critical Inquiry* (Summer
1998), Brown writes, "*Homebase* . . . offers a basic lesson in
how, despite the purported mass-cultural homogenization of
America in the 1950s, some products, significantly recoded,

could become the ground from which to express ethnic indi-viduation." Brown is referring to the scene in the novel where Rainsford learns Chinese from a ventriloquist doll. Discuss why this scene is in the novel and how that scene further compli-cates who is narrating the story. What other emblems or sym-bols of American culture are in the novel?

8

In the same essay by Bill Brown, he goes on to write, "Psychic survival [in *Homebase*] depends on saturating the object world with significance." Discuss how the structure of *Homebase* proves his point.

9

When *Homebase* was published in 1979, it was the only novel by a Chinese American author in print in America at the time. Knowing this while writing the novel, Shawn Wong had the responsibility of not only telling a story, but also of educating a reading audience to Chinese American literature and his-tory. If the story were published today, do you think the author would've approached the telling of the story differently?

10

If you have seen the Bill Moyers PBS documentary, *Becoming American: The Chinese Experience* (2003), compare and contrast how the documentary and *Homebase* define the idea of "becoming American."

11

Throughout the novel, Rainsford's search for his identity is very much rooted in finding a sense of home. How do his journeys through different geographical locations, and his naming of places from the summit of Shasta to the mountain at the end, form the progression that eventually leads to his acceptance of his identity? (Professor Stephanie Wells, Orange Coast College)

12

One of the most striking things about *Homebase* is the way the narrative voice, originally Rainsford's, seamlessly shifts in and out of the identities and experiences of his father, grandfather, and great-grandfather; in fact, Rainsford describes his journey as "mov[ing] across America picking up ghosts." How does this narrative choice enhance our reading of Rainsford's journey? What's the symbolic function of this narrative slippage? (Professor Stephanie Wells, Orange Coast College)

13

The novel contains two female romantic love interests for Rainsford, neither of whom is named; one is the fifteen-year-old "blond body" who represents "the true dream of [his] capture of

America," while the other is a Chinese American woman whom he has only known briefly and who only appears in memory. Which of the two, if either, plays the greater role in allowing him to affirm his American identity, and must his identity be affirmed or denied by or through a woman? (Professor Stephanie Wells, Orange Coast College)

14

How does "the blond body" function as a symbol for Rainsford? Do you read her as being a literal person, or a construct of his imagination? (Professor Stephanie Wells, Orange Coast College)

15

Look up some examples of Angel Island poetry at www.angel island.org. After reading the poems written by the Chinese immigrants, can you identify ways in which these poets are also concerned with the notion of place as a marker of identity? (Professor Stephanie Wells, Orange Coast College)